Anne Boleyn

The Final 24 Hours

Marcella Mayfair

The Prophecy

When the Tower is white, and another place green,
Then shall be burned two or three bishops and a queen.
And after all this be passed we shall have a merry world.

The prophecy of the Abbot of Garadon

4:50AM 18ᵗʰ May 1536

The Queen's Lodgings - The Tower of London

Just over four hours until the scheduled time of Anne Boleyn's execution.

Anne Boleyn is nearing the end of hearing Mass.

The service is being conducted by her friend and longtime confidante the Archbishop of Canterbury, Thomas Cranmer, who has arrived from Lambeth Palace specifically for the task.

Also present are her ladies: Margaret Wyatt, a woman she has known since childhood Katherine Carey, her 12-year-old niece; Lady Boleyn; Elizabeth Wood, her aunt; and Mrs Mary Orchard, her one-time nurse. Her almoner, John Skip, is also in attendance. Both he and Anne have been praying since two of the clock after midnight. Mass, followed by her final confession, is the natural conclusion to the process of preparing her soul for immortality.

Also present, at the specific request of Anne, is Sir William Kingston, Constable of the Tower.

Kingston is feeling weary and not just because of the earliness of the hour.

He is approaching sixty years of age and has been Constable of the Tower for twelve years. He has fought wars side by side with the Duke of Suffolk and has loyally served the king in a variety of capacities ever since Henry came to the throne as a teenage boy. He might venture so far as to consider the king a friend.

Yet nothing has aged him like the events of the previous fortnight.

Until recently he had been responsible for the imprisonment of six men accused of committing the vilest of acts with the Queen of England. Just yesterday morning he accompanied five of them, Henry Norris, Francis Weston, William Brereton, Mark Smeaton and the queen's brother, Lord Rochford on the short journey to Tower Hill. There, in front of the London crowd, an executioner supplied by the city removed their heads with an axe according to the judgements that had been delivered against them.

Kingston's important charges were suddenly much reduced in number.

One man still remained in the Tower. Thomas Wyatt, brother of Margaret who was currently serving the queen. He had not yet been sent to trial. But the rumour around court was that it was surely just a matter of time, and no one had any doubt as to what his fate would be.

At the start of the month, on the 2nd of May, Kingston had been requested to attend court. This was not an unusual event for Kingston. He attended court on a regular basis and was on very good terms with the king. Yet something was strange that day. There was talk of arrests amongst both the king's and queen's households. People were walking the corridors in fear. There was also the matter of the king's sudden departure from the previous day's May Jousts. With his years of experience in political dealings, Kingston knew something significant was occurring.

And so he was proven correct.

He was summoned to a secret meeting with the king's Chief Minister, Thomas Cromwell. During the meeting he received orders to hurriedly prepare the queen's apartments at the Tower. The queen was coming to stay; she would be arriving by barge later that day. This was not the same as her previous stay in the apartments. Then, she had awaited the joyful event of her coronation. Today, she would be lodging as the king's prisoner. Kingston was also instructed by Cromwell to keep a close watch on Anne's demeanour and to record, in detail, any talk of significance. This was to be reported back to him on a daily basis as a minimum. If something important was mentioned, then it was to be reported immediately. In order to aid Kingston in his spying endeavour, Lady Boleyn was placed as one of those to serve upon the queen. Cromwell also requested that Lady Kingston spend as much time as possible with the prisoner. The ladies in question would report to Kingston who would, in turn, submit his report to Cromwell.

Kingston duly hurried back to the Tower to take control of the situation.

After seeing that the arrangements regarding her accommodation had been carried out satisfactorily, Kingston was present at the arrival of the queen and greeted her with due respect, at which point Anne enquired if she should be placed in a dungeon. Kingston assured her that her own apartments had been made up for her and that she would be lodging there. She retorted that it was too good for her. Then she burst into a bout of hysterical laughter which quite unnerved Kingston and sent a shiver down his spine. On recovering her composure, the queen enquired as to whether Kingston was aware of the reason behind her imprisonment. Kingston confirmed in all honesty that he was not. Anne furthered her questioning of her custodian, asking when he had last seen the king. Kingston replied that he had not seen him since his appearance at the May Day jousts. She asked about her brother George and her father. Kingston gave her truthful answers where he could on their whereabouts. Anne then commented on the rumours that she would be tried with three men. Kingston told her that he could not comment on this matter. Quite simply he had no idea himself what was occurring.

Before the two parted, Anne asked Kingston a final, searching question. "Master Kingston," she asked. "Am I going to die without justice?" Kingston replied that even the poorest subject in the kingdom had justice.

Anne simply laughed at Kingston's answer in the same hysterical manner that had become commonplace over the last two weeks.

The next morning Kingston reported the full detail of this conversation in a communication that he rushed to Thomas Cromwell. It was the first of many such letters.

Over the next days Kingston was made responsible for arranging suitable accommodation for the trial of the two currently held in the tower, namely the Queen and her brother. The trial was set for the 15th of May and the Tower had to be made available for the peers of the land who had come to pass judgement on the prisoners. With so much happening and so many great men in attendance, the people within the Tower's mighty buttresses had to be managed. There was talk of terrible scandal, wickedness, adultery and incest throughout London. People naturally gravitated towards the Tower to be close to the centre of intrigue.

For Kingston it was a logistical nightmare without precedence.

After the judgement was passed, which incidentally was guilty and was unanimous (even Thomas Boleyn found his own children guilty), Kingston had to arrange for a suitable scaffold to be built within the precinct of the Tower. Word had been sent that the queen would not burn as the original sentence had decreed. The king had graciously commuted the sentence to a mere be-heading, thus sparing his former wife (an annulment had already been issued) the horrors of a death by fire. There were also instructions of a further concession. The executioner of the Tower would not be required. Instead, the famed executioner of Calais, who used a sword as opposed to an axe, had already been sent for and had been lodging within the Tower since the previous evening. How word had managed to be sent and the swordsman managed to arrive in London with such speed was a mystery to Kingston.

The only conclusion he could come to was that the executioner had been sent for before Anne Boleyn's trial had even taken place. He had already decided that he wouldn't ask Cromwell for clarification regarding this matter. The king's business was the king's business.

So his exhaustion while he watched Anne Boleyn take her last sacrament was understandable. He half wondered why the queen had requested him to be present at this very private affair. But in reality he knew the answer.

Anne was clever. Her wit was one of the qualities that first attracted the king. Anne knew that Kingston was reporting everything directly to Cromwell and possibly even to the king. She wanted them to know that she was behaving with the utmost dignity and that she wasn't in floods of tears confessing her guilt.

Kingston longed for this all to be over. Retirement was long overdue. Once this sorry affair was concluded, that would be high on his agenda.

Yet Anne Boleyn still had one more hand to play against Kingston that morning.

After Mass was concluded she declared that she was going to give her final confession to the Archbishop. This was completely normal; anyone preparing for imminent death would do the same. The soul needed to be purged of its sins in preparation for taking its place in heaven. What wasn't normal was to request someone else be present at that confession. Yet Anne very boldly requested that Kingston remain to hear her confession to Cranmer.

His first instinct was to refuse.

But he knew that within four hours the queen would be walking up the stairs of the scaffold and he needed her to be calm. His first rule when dealing with important prisoners was that they needed to be kept calm. It would not look good for him if the queen went to her death in hysterics because he refused a simple request.

Kingston agreed.

He knelt quietly as she confessed that she was sorry for any offence she may have given the king, although not with her body.

Kingston knew why he was there. He was to report that in her final confession the Queen had not confessed to the crimes of which she had been found guilty. In fact, she specifically had said they did not occur.

He wasn't sure what or who to believe. He could not accept that a woman would not confess of her sins when the opportunity was available to her. And yet he did not want to believe that she was about to be executed for a crime she did not commit. One of the two situations had to be the case and yet Kingston was not sure which was the most repugnant.

5:00AM 18th May 1536

The residence of Thomas Cromwell, London

Four hours until the scheduled time of Anne Boleyn's execution.

Thomas Cromwell, Henry VIII's chief minister, is at his desk. He is always at work by this hour, a habit that he learned from his old master, the Cardinal. However, the previous night he slept little and had arisen at 3:30 to begin work.

He is attempting to put matters in the Tower at the back of his mind for an hour or two in order to attend to important matters of state. It is difficult.

Over the past month his time has been consumed with the investigation, trial, and now, execution of the queen. It was the greatest and the most important gamble of his life. If he had lost, then more than likely it would have been him awaiting the touch of steel on his bare neck that morning.

The queen's hostility towards him had been growing since the end of the previous year. Fortunately for Cromwell it corresponded with the growing dissatisfaction that the king felt towards his queen. Ever the manipulator, Cromwell was able to use this to his advantage. Over the last month, with a combination of cunning, lies, scandal and brutality, Cromwell had smashed the Boleyn faction at court into oblivion. Some of them had already met their fate. Within a few hours there would be no figurehead left for those that remained to gather around.

Cromwell had felt some regret. After all, the queen had been his champion and to a certain degree he had been hers, at least in the early days.

But Cromwell knew that nothing stays still. Not in this world. Certainly not at the court of Henry VIII.

He had no option, it was a case of survival. Her or him. Both could not have the ear of the king.

Here, within these very walls, he managed to get a confession out of young Master Mark. A confession so scandalous, so shocking, that the world would believe anything else that Cromwell said had happened. Cromwell took advantage of this and he said that much happened between the queen and various gentlemen of court. Very few voiced doubt over the claims.

Soon it would be over. The king had already issued instructions for Cromwell to plan his wedding to Mistress Seymour. It was just another matter that he had to attend to. The monasteries continued to be closed, there were reports on various submissions for his attention that had been left unread and unanswered. There were the usual requests for a share of the spoils over these closures, all supported by pages of documents. Pensions for fat abbots that had already submitted had to be confirmed. There were pages and pages of legal requests of one type or another. Another pile of documents consisted of reports from his Majesty's ambassadors across Europe. Then there were the reports from Cromwell's various spies in England and beyond. There were the building progress reports from the various projects in many of the king's palaces. Many of these were lagging behind and Cromwell had to find the time to issue rebukes and demands to get the works back on track. Then there were reports from the naval yards on the construction of the great warships. Then the various correspondence from important personages, including the Lady Mary, the Imperial Ambassador, Cranmer. The list went on and on and on. Being the chief minister of the king brought a workload that would break any normal man.

But all of these matters had been on hold while Cromwell masterminded the downfall of the queen.

Very soon it would be over.

Cromwell would then be able to breathe a sigh of relief.

He picks up another report from the top of the nearest pile and begins to read.

6:02 AM 18ᵗʰ May 1536

The Bell Tower, The Tower of London

Less than three hours until the scheduled time of Anne Boleyn's execution.

Thomas Wyatt cannot sleep.

Yesterday he witnessed, from the window of his room in the tower, the deaths of five men on Tower Hill. He knew from his guards that these were the men that had been tried and convicted of committing adultery with the queen. These were all men that he knew. In some cases, men that he was friends with. He had watched as one by one they addressed the crown and then laid their necks on the block before the executioner brought down the axe and a swift end to their treachery.

He too was imprisoned on suspicion of adultery with the queen. And yet he had not met the same fate. He was not guilty of the crime, that much was true. However, he was not convinced that those executed yesterday were guilty either, and yet still they walked to their deaths. He had loved the woman once; everyone knew that to be the case. So much so that he requested the king send him abroad so that he could escape her power. But would he be stupid enough to commit adultery with the Queen of England? That would be pure folly.

He had been questioned by Cromwell himself and he had vigorously denied the allegation. Despite his incarceration, Cromwell, who had always been friendly towards him, had hinted that he would be good to him and that he should not give himself to great concern.

Cromwell never showed his hand to anyone and Wyatt was left guessing just what he meant. However, he strongly suspected that, because the king was aware of his earlier affection for the lady, he too had to be questioned. He prayed each day that he could trust Cromwell and that the king wouldn't be hasty in his quest for vengeance.

He was housed comfortably enough. And he had his pens and papers with him. He had composed a few lines when his mind was able.

He was staring at a few that he had just written:

These bloody days have broken my heart.
My lust, my youth did them depart,
And blind desire of estate.
Who hastes to climb seeks to revert.
Of truth, circa Regna tonat.

He knew he could use them somewhere, in something. As long as he was able to get through this with his head still on his shoulders.

He simply had to take Cromwell to be as good as his word… and he knew that was a very dangerous thing to do.

6:50AM 18ᵗʰ May 1536

The River Thames, London

Two hours and 10 minutes until the scheduled time of Anne Boleyn's execution.

Archbishop Cranmer is being rowed back to Lambeth Palace, tears are flowing down his face.

He couldn't bear to witness the execution. He was relieved that Anne did not ask it of him.

It was an emotional parting. She had pressed a small brooch into his hand. It was of little value she said, as her expensive items had been retained by the king. But it was something to remember her by. She had told him not to cry for her because later she would be in heaven and at peace.

But he couldn't help but cry. The great champion of the reformers was about to meet her fate. It seemed only fitting.

7:00 AM 18ᵗʰ May 1536

The Queen's Lodgings, The Tower of London

Two hours till the scheduled time of Anne Boleyn's execution.

Anne is calm.

In two hours she would be released from the emotional turmoil that had been driving her insane for the last two weeks. She was glad of it. She did not wish for death, but above all she desired for her tormented mind to be at rest. She also had the solace that when in heaven she would see her beloved brother again.

When she miscarried her final child, her boy, the king's heir, in January she knew that her husband was slipping away from her. She knew that if she lost the protection of her husband the predators who were always out there would look for the right moment to strike.

She had made many enemies on her meteoric rise to become the king's queen. Some of these enemies, like Wolsey, she had managed to defeat on route, but there were many others that were still waiting. Suffolk, Richmond, the Lady Mary – the list of those that wished her ill was long. Now, at the head of that list, was Thomas Cromwell, the man she had helped raise from his lowly position as Wolsey's man.

Then there was the problem of the Seymour girl. She had been ready for weeks to pounce at the slightest weakness. She knew how that felt; she had been there herself. Yet she was confused as to how the stupid little

Seymour girl had gotten the king so excited. Henry had bedded other women during their marriage, of course. When she had confronted him about it, he told her that she should shut up and endure it like her betters had done before her. That simple sentence was a double blow to her pride. After all of the waiting and all of the heartache to get rid of Katherine, now Henry implied that she was her better. Now there was this new danger. This Seymour girl was different from the normal women he took to his bed, and yet the queen considered her plain. Anne knew perfectly well that queens could be removed and she rather suspected that Jane had her beady little eyes on her crown. Her fears of the infatuation of her husband were confirmed when she saw the stupid girl wearing a gift from the king, an expensive necklace with his portrait in a fine locket.

Day by day, piece by piece, Henry was lost to her. He didn't come to her bed. He shunned her. Humiliated her.

But then suddenly there was hope. Henry had played an elaborate game in which he tricked the Imperial Ambassador to acknowledge her in public. After three years the king was triumphant and Anne basked in the glory. Finally, an acknowledgement had come from Spain that she was the true queen. Maybe it was a turning point? Maybe Henry would love her again.

But then in the middle of the May Day jousts he leapt to his feet and was gone. He rode off without a word or a backward glance.

Anne knew at that moment something was very wrong.

She was right. Within a day she was arrested and brought to the Tower.

She had written to Henry and appealed to his chivalric nature. But there was no response. No acknowledgement. She was abandoned to her fate.

The charges against her, when they were finally presented, were so absurd they were laughable. Adultery with five gentlemen? All on more than one occasion? One man not even fit to be considered a gentleman? On her own dear brother? Would she really risk the fires of hell by committing the abomination of incest? The peers that stood in judgement of her clearly thought she would, as they all without hesitation, stood and pronounced her guilty of the crimes of which she had been accused. She could see her uncle's face now as he passed the sentence upon her. As he had spoken the fateful words Suffolk had been at his side, smiling wryly at his revenge.

Despite the falseness of the accusations and the injustice of it all, she was determined that she would go to her death with dignity. She would not give her enemies the pleasure of seeing her break down.

Her peace with God was made. He knew she was innocent of the crimes of which she was accused. Of course, she also knew that she was guilty of other crimes, her treatment of Lady Mary for one. For that she knew that she deserved to die.

But she would die with dignity.

She calls her maids and begins to dress for one final time.

7:15AM 18th May 1536
The residence of Thomas Cromwell, London

One hour and 45 minutes until the scheduled time of Anne Boleyn's execution.

Cromwell has been troubled since he awoke. Despite his best efforts he has not been able to concentrate on the mass of documents that need his attention.

He knows that not enough thought has gone into what is going to occur in the Tower that morning.

The desire for a swift end to this unprecedented situation has resulted in an execution that may well appear to the world to be nothing more than a murder. It has occurred to him that he cannot risk having foreign witnesses present at the Tower. The ambassadors will all have sent their men, or may even attend themselves. He certainly wouldn't put it past Eustace Chapuys, the Imperial Ambassador, to watch the death of the woman he hated. If something were to go wrong, or the lady cry out her innocence, then the king's reputation would be badly damaged overseas. He has already received a number of reports from the continent since the queen's arrest: he knows that Henry and his queen are the talk of Europe. The European courts are amazed at the happenings in England. Cromwell needs to protect his master's name.

He hurriedly writes an order to Kingston at the Tower.

7:25AM 18ᵗʰ May 1536

Whitehall Palace

One hour and 35 minutes until the scheduled time of Anne Boleyn's execution.

His Majesty King Henry VIII of England, supreme head of the Church of England on Earth, is hearing Mass.

He is a devout and highly religious man and today of all days was a day to be conversing with God.

With him are some of his closest and oldest companions and relations.

The Duke of Suffolk, Charles Brandon, his brother-in-law, was the closest to his king. His father had been struck down at Bosworth holding the king's father's banner high. He had been in a place of high honour at the Tudor court ever since. Suffolk had not complained about the downfall of the queen; in fact, he was relishing every moment. His wife, before her death was very close to Queen Katherine and, of course, the Lady Mary who shared her name. She had fought in Katherine's corner with her brother whenever she could, even leaving court in protest at his treatment of her. Suffolk shared his dead wife's disparaging views on Anne Boleyn. He, along with others in the chapel that morning, had virtually pushed Jane Seymour in the king's direction. Suffolk was fully aware of talk that the king was unable to produce male children. He knew it to be absurd: it was the queen who had been at fault. God willing, the new Queen Jane would be able to provide the king with an heir.

Obviously the king was able to sire male children, because also present was the Duke of Richmond and Somerset, Henry Fitzroy. Richmond was Henry's illegitimate son with his long time mistress Elizabeth Blount. In the absence of a legitimate heir the king had heaped titles and offices on his bastard. Like Suffolk, the young Duke of Richmond would shed no tears for the queen that morning. So fearful was she that Richmond would usurp the rights of her daughter, Elizabeth, that many believed that she would result to poison to remove him. Richmond had begun to feel a little unwell recently, but he put it down to being caught in an unexpected hail storm while hunting and catching a chill. At the same time, the fear of the queen's poison had always been at the back of his mind. The swordsman would soon stop that worry and he wasn't sorry a bit.

Sir Francis Bryan, gentleman of the king's bedchamber, is also in attendance at Mass. He had been away from court when the queen was suddenly arrested. Cromwell summoned him back in haste. In fact, Bryan had been subjected to a rather uncomfortable interview by Cromwell and Sir William Fitzwilliam as part of their investigation into the lewd behaviour of the queen. Bryan had once been a well-known Boleyn man, but in recent months he too had moved over to the Seymour faction. Bryan couldn't help but think that if he had answered Cromwell's questions slightly differently, then he too might have ended up in the Tower. He was now the king's sounding board for his anger against Anne. For the past few evenings Henry has been entertaining a string of young, attractive women. Bryan believes it is Henry's reaction to the very public revelation that his queen has made him a cuckold. The king must prove his manliness to his court and country once again. Bryan didn't object for a moment and became a very willing companion in the king's games.

Henry is trying his best to put the lady that had bewitched him for so long out of his mind. He is finding it hard, the pain of her betrayal is still raw. He sets his mind on the future and Jane. Jane has been lodging elsewhere as the scandal erupts around court. It was best to keep her out of the way so that she would not have her name compromised with unsavoury allegations while the queen was imprisoned. He decides that he needs a change of environment; he had been locked within the palace since this whole affair engulfed his world. Tonight he would dine with Jane and her family. Henry realised that he missed her. It would be a merry occasion. He would look forward to it.

He stared without looking as the priest held up the host.

He wanted Anne's face out of his mind. He wanted to hear the cannon. He wanted to know it was over.

7:40 AM 18ᵗʰ May 1536

The Queen's Lodgings - The Tower of London

1 hour and 20 minutes until the scheduled time of Anne Boleyn's execution.

Anne is dressed for her final walk. She has told all her ladies that she will meet her fate like a true queen.

She attempts to read passages from the Bible, but her mind keeps flicking to another matter.

Her daughter.

What would become of Elizabeth?

She knew how she had forced Henry to act towards the Lady Mary. Would the stupid Seymour girl force Henry to act in the same manner to Elizabeth? Mary had at least been a woman and could offer residence. Elizabeth was just a defenseless child with no comprehension of what was occurring. She would be swallowed up in the political fallout that would follow her death. Who would protect her? Her father? She doubted it. Her father would do as he had always done and protect himself. Her sister Mary? She regretted that she had never reconciled herself fully with her sister. She had summoned Katherine to act as one of her maids and sent Mary some gifts, but she had not gone so far as to welcome her back to court. Elizabeth would be alone, unless Henry decided to be the father he never was to Mary.

She had obviously wished for a boy. But in the years since Elizabeth's birth she had come to envisage her sitting on the throne of England in her own right as Henry's one true heir. She doubted that would happen now. The best she could hope for was a halfhearted advantageous match with some son of a leading noble, maybe some second son of a European Prince. Elizabeth wasn't Henry's heir any longer, just his little bastard.

She just had to pray that Elizabeth would overcome the trials that would undoubtedly be put before her.

It was a lot to pray for.

7:45 AM 18ᵗʰ May 1536

Heaver Castle, Kent

1 hour and 15 minutes until the scheduled time of Anne Boleyn's execution.

Elizabeth Boleyn was inconsolable.

She had been in bed for the last two days, ever since she had arrived from London. Her maids had not been able to offer any form of comfort. She couldn't sleep, she wouldn't eat, and try as she might she didn't really wish to still be breathing. Her distraught nature did little to help her terrible cough which had been raging for the best part of two months. Death was approaching, she knew it. She just wished it would come quickly and release her from her torment.

Like the rest of the court she was stunned with the speed of her family's downfall.

How she had basked in the glory that she was the Queen of England's mother. Oh yes, she had enjoyed that. The fact that people would go out of their way to offer her a kind word or a gift. Requests for favours were not uncommon. Finally, after all of these years, she was an important woman.

She had been a little upset when she, the daughter of the Duke of Norfolk no less, was married off to a man as low as Thomas Boleyn. However, as her father explained somewhat bluntly, with the reputation that she had at court it was difficult to get her someone better. No one at court was under any illusions that Lady Elizabeth

Howard, as she was then, was a virgin. Or anything close to being a virgin. So Thomas Boleyn would have to do. He was ambitious enough and her father was convinced that he would come to good fortune.

She had lived a comfortable if unremarkable life, until her brother, the new Duke of Norfolk, came up with the idea of dangling her daughters in front of the king in order to gain favour. The eldest, Mary, had been the first to grace Henry's bed. He wasn't the only king she had slept with: The King of France made her his lover during her time in the French court. People whispered names behind her back, calling her the great and infamous whore. Mistress to two kings — it was unheard of. Some said that she was just like her mother. Her mother disagreed. Mary couldn't have been that "great" because she failed to keep Henry's interest for long, and he had discarded her. No one had ever discarded Elizabeth Howard! However, Anne fared somewhat better. As opposed to following her sister's route to his bed, she kept refusing him, driving him wild with desire in the process. Finally, after breaking from the clutches of Rome, Henry annulled his marriage to his queen of over twenty years in order to wed her younger daughter.

She had watched in silent triumph as they placed the crown on Anne's head in Westminster Abbey. She was the mother of the queen. Finally, her importance in this world had been recognised.

But now all was lost.

Her beloved George, her handsome young man, was dead. She had received word that very morning that he had died on Tower Hill the previous day. She was overcome with grief. She had lost many children in infancy or birth, but those losses were expected. No one expects to lose a child to the executioner's axe. Then there was Anne, who would meet the same fate, it seemed. Elizabeth could not feel the same regret about her daughter as she could for her son. If only Anne had kept Henry happy, then all of this would never have happened. If Anne had learnt to keep silent and be a sweet, loving, demure wife, if Anne hadn't lost that boy earlier this year, then this would never have happened. Anne was to blame.

Now all she had left was a daughter whom she had disowned. A stupid girl who, despite the fact her sister was queen, decided to marry for love. She could enjoy the love and the poverty that went with it. Elizabeth would never forgive her.

What further horrors awaited? Would her husband now follow his children to the scaffold? If that were to happen then the riches they enjoyed would be given up to the crown. What would it mean for her? Insignificance and obscurity, that was what it would mean.

Everything was lost.

8:40AM 18ᵗʰ May 1536

The Constables' Lodgings, The Tower of London.

20 minutes until the scheduled time of Anne Boleyn's execution.

Ralph Sadler arrives at the Tower and immediately demands to see Kingston. Knowing that he is Cromwell's man he is immediately admitted.

Sadler hands Kingston a message with Cromwell's personal seal. The message tells Kingston not to proceed with the execution until all strangers have been removed from the Tower. Cromwell explains that he is concerned of what might happen if there is a problem with the execution. Were ambassadors or agents of foreign powers to witness the events, they would not paint a flattering picture of the king overseas.

Kingston is annoyed that there is to be a delay to the matter at hand. In his mind, the sooner the deed is done, the better. However, he cannot fault Cromwell's reasoning: the king's reputation overseas must be protected at all costs. He simply wishes that Cromwell had given his instructions earlier. Despite his feelings, he is skilled enough in matters of statecraft to not let these frustrations show to Sadler.

Kingston tells Sadler that he will delay the execution until at least noon, by which time the strangers will have been removed. He requests that, for the avoidance of doubt, Cromwell provide him with a suitable time for proceeding with the execution so that any essential witnesses may be present. He also tells Sadler that he has an interesting report for Cromwell regarding events earlier in the day; however, he has not yet had time to write it and it will thus follow at the earliest opportunity.

Sadler rides off to report back to Cromwell.

Kingston summons Sir Edmund Walsingham, his deputy, from where he is directing matters close to the scaffold site. Walsingham is stunned to hear the execution is to be delayed. The two men hurriedly decide on the best course of action in order to fulfil the task set to them.

Walsingham leaves and delegates the actual responsibility for clearing the tower of the strangers and foreigners with The Sheriff of London, Richard Gresham, who is already at the Tower to witness the execution. He leaves Gresham to the task and goes to inform the guards at the open gate that no foreigners are to be granted access from this moment forward.

Kingston summons his wife and begins writing his report to Cromwell regarding Anne's non-admission of guilt at her confession.

8:45 AM 18ᵗʰ May 1536

The Queen's Lodgings - The Tower of London

15 minutes until the scheduled time of Anne Boleyn's execution.

The atmosphere in the Queen's lodgings is becoming tense. Each little sound turns everyone's head towards the door.

"I am ready," Anne declares in frustration to no one in particular. "I trust that Mister Kingston shall arrive shortly; indeed, I had expected him already."

That was the feeling of everyone in the room. Everyone wanted this to be over.

Where was Kingston?

8:47AM 18th May 1536

The Residence of the Imperial Ambassador, London

13 minutes until the scheduled time of Anne Boleyn's execution

Despite the pain, Eustace Chapuys is in a triumphant mood.

Ever since news of the concubine's sentence he has been deliberating whether he should attend the execution. His heart felt that he should. After all, she had been his mortal enemy since the moment he arrived on English soil. The horrors she had committed against the person of the blessed Queen Katherine were almost unspeakable. How she had manipulated and twisted the once honourable King with her whorish French ways and caused him to risk his immortal soul by breaking from the guidance of the Holy Father was devilishness in the extreme. When he thinks of Katherine in her final moments — alone, impoverished, and without the love of her husband or daughter — he knows that he should be in attendance to watch the axe fall. He should be close enough to see the fear in the whore's eyes.

If nothing else, he should be the one to present a personal account of the events to the Princess Mary who had received just as harsh treatment as her mother at the concubine's hands. With the woman's death the princess would be free from the fear of poisoning that she had suffered. Could there now be the chance of a reconciliation between the princess and her father?

Would Henry himself now crawl back to the bosom of Rome?

Henry, though, had at present another bosom in mind.

Chapuys knew little of the Seymour girl's religious affiliations. Other than the fact that she was vaguely pleasing to the eye, he knew little about her at all. The girl's father, John, was a mere knight and had publicly shamed himself with a younger woman some years before. That little titbit of gossip his spies did manage to find out. Her brothers, Edward and Thomas, were both highly ambitious. He had spoken to Edward on occasion and found him both deliberate and calculating. With the favour of the king behind him, he would likely make a good politician. Edward Seymour was certainly a man to watch and befriend: he was a rising star who would go far. He had no dealings with the younger brother, Thomas. Yet he didn't need his spies to tell him that he was one of the new, flamboyant young men at court. Good looks and money meant that he bedded maidens for sport. A little digging brought forth stories of drunken brawls and gambling debts. Thomas Seymour was a hot headed youth who no doubt would now be placed in a position of importance completely unsuitable for him. But about Jane herself, he had found out little. During her time as a lady in waiting to the concubine she behaved impeccably. Other than the king, there appeared to have been no other man. It seemed that her willingness to succumb to the king's advances started the avalanche that had engulfed her former mistress. Maybe she would be sympathetic to Princess Mary's cause?

Despite feeling that he should be at the Tower that morning, there were other considerations.

Firstly, the king. He had been playing a game with Henry for years now, refusing to acknowledge his whore as his queen or his bastard daughter as his heir. Yet just a matter of weeks ago Henry had managed to corner him at chapel. He, Ambassador to his Imperial Majesty, found himself face to face with the concubine herself. With much of the court and the king watching, he had little choice but to acknowledge her with a bow. On that occasion she had been the one triumphant. Finally, an acknowledgement all be it small, from Spain. Now, just days later, the positions were reversed. But how would Henry respond to his presence at the Tower? He would know that he was there to report every detail to his master and Princess Mary. Would this anger Henry? The king's behaviour had been erratic of late. Who knew how he would behave?

Then there was his own dread. Despite the fact he was joyful that his enemy had finally been cast down, he was not filled with delight at seeing her head smitten from her body. He had avoided executions in the past. He had seen them in his homeland in his youth. Burnings. The thought made his stomach crawl even now. Losing the contents of his stomach in front of the assembled witnesses would make him a laughing stock.

Finally, there was something else. Despite the feeling of triumph, despite the desire in his heart for vengeance, there was something else. The concubine's trial had been nothing but a sham. No witnesses were even called to provide evidence; she was allowed no defence. The lady was convicted on nothing more than hearsay and the lewd gossip of spiteful people. It was a political coup, pure and simple.

How did he feel that a woman, even one such as the concubine, would be put to death on such terms?

He had wrestled with his choice. Attend? Stay away?

Matters were taken out of his hands the night before when pain engulfed his toe and ankle, making it impossible to stand. The situation had not improved this morning. The physician had been summoned and had informed him that it was a case of gout. He had never had such a thing before and the pain was such that he could not even bear the bed sheet to lay against his infected toe. Wine and cherries were the recommended treatment. Wine he had. But where he could get cherries in London in the month of May he didn't know.

So this was why he was in bed that morning and not at the Tower. He had compromised and sent his man to watch proceedings unfold and he was under orders to rush straight back and give a full account.

He would wait.

The sound of the cannon from the wharf would tell him that Queen Katherine had been avenged.

But he knew that how it was done was going to be a travesty of justice.

9:10AM 18ᵗʰ May 1536

The Queen's Lodgings - The Tower of London

10 minutes after the scheduled time for the execution

Anne Boleyn is nervously pacing the room.

She is dressed simply in a plain black kirtle. A robe trimmed with ermine fur awaits in the hands of Mary Orchard who is standing close to the door. Anne clutches her prayer book close to her chest in a vice-like grip. In the far corner John Skip is reading out Bible verses regarding the resurrection in a low, reassuring voice that anyone can easily talk over. Anne complains loudly to Lady Boleyn that the appointed hour has come and gone and she had expected to be with her brother in paradise. Why was it not so? Lady Boleyn offers no reply other than a simple shrug of her shoulders. She knows nothing and, like everyone else in the room, wishes it were all over. John Skip continues his verses as though Anne had never spoken in the first place, and everyone is listening as though he were preaching a sermon.

Margaret Wyatt and Katherine Carey look as nervous as the queen. Katherine looks close to tears and wishes that she didn't have to fulfil this final duty for her aunt. Anne looks at the two younger women and offers a reassuring smile. "Remember your dignity out there," she reminds them. They nod and try to compose themselves. Neither wish to let their mistress down in her final moments.

Footsteps are heard outside in the corridor and everyone looks expectantly at the door as it is opened.

Lady Kingston enters and immediately everyone is aware that this isn't what was expected. Anne speaks before Lady Kingston has time to open her mouth, "Madam, where is your husband? I had presumed him to accompany me on this final journey."

Lady Kingston pauses. She has no love for the woman that she faces. She knew the terrible things that Anne had done to blessed Queen Katherine and her poor child the Lady Mary. Lady Kingston was particularly friendly with the Lady Mary and she was fully aware of the threats, the humiliation and, if the rumours were true, the poison that Anne threw in her direction. It had been a pleasure to write the secret reports of her downfall and her state of mind during her imprisonment, to Eustace Chapuys, the Spanish Ambassador. So much of a pleasure in fact, that she almost didn't take the coin he paid her to be his spy. Almost.

Despite the hatred that flows through her veins, as she sees the desperation in Anne's eyes she can't help but feel twinges of pity.

She clears her throat and delivers the news that the deed would not now be undertaken until sometime after noon.

Anne objects to the delay with a frantic passion. She tells everyone that she is ready for death. She repeats what they already know, that she had been preparing for it since two hours after midnight. She demands to know the reason for the delay. Lady Kingston replies that she does not know the full details but an order has been received by her husband to delay matters.

Silence fills the room.

Where there had been just despair in the mind of Anne now there was something else.

Hope.

Not much, but finally, after a pit of darkness for the past two weeks, there is a flicker of light.

A thousand thoughts run through her mind.

Had the king relented? Had it all been some form of test? Maybe he was even now travelling up the Thames on his royal barge to release her from this madness himself? Once again she would be his queen.

But it could not be. Five men had perished. She had watched her own brother's head be hacked from his broad shoulders.

Once Henry's mind was decided, it could not be deviated. Her own rise to power was testament to that.

Yet what if it had been a mistake? What if Cromwell had been behind it all and now that Henry had discovered what was occurring he was putting a halt to it?

Her mind is torn. Although she does not desire death, Anne knows that she has prepared herself well for it. A delay could loosen her resolve to face the swordsman with bravery and courage. But if there is hope? Hope that she may see her beautiful daughter again? Hope that she may sit at Henry's table and share his bed?

Lady Kingston leaves to inform her husband that the prisoner has been told of the delay.

9:15AM 18th May 1536

Tower Green

15 minutes after the scheduled time of Anne Boleyn's execution

Richard Gresham is explaining to a man that he must leave the Tower. The man is either pretending not to understand or is just being difficult. Gresham has managed to establish that this is Eustace Chapuys' man. But trying to get through to him that he must leave is proving almost impossible. The fact that he is the servant of the Imperial Ambassador is making it a little more difficult. Politeness is key.

Gresham has with him one of his own men, a Mister William Cooke. Cooke doesn't do politeness that well. He is, however, particularly good at offering brawn where it is required.

Finally, Gresham manages to get the message to the man that he has to leave. The man looks most agitated that he will not be able to provide a report on the events to his master. For the sake of ensuring the man actually leaves the Tower he instructs Cooke to accompany him to the gate.

Taking a long look at Cooke, the Ambassador's man decides that he will go quickly and without further protest.

9:43AM 18ᵗʰ May 1536

The Queen's Lodgings - The Tower of London

43 minutes after the scheduled time of Anne Boleyn's execution

After a period of silent reflection on the news brought by Lady Kingston, Anne talks quietly with Mary Orchard in hushed tones so the other women, and in particular Lady Boleyn, cannot hear. She suddenly leaps to her feet and demands to see the Constable of the Tower.

Despite their best efforts, her ladies are unable to comfort her and Lady Boleyn is dispatched to fetch Kingston.

Kingston arrives looking harried, with Lady Boleyn in his wake. He greets Anne with a bow which she promptly ignores.

"Master Kingston. I am told that I will not now die before noon. I had longed to be out of my pain by now," she says.

"Madam. There will be no pain," Kingston replies. "The executioner is very good."

Anne reaches up and places both her hands around her bare neck, "And I have such a little neck." She then breaks into another fit of her hysterical laughter.

Everyone watches her with concern, wondering if madness will take her before the executioner's sword.

Kingston offers his apologies for the delay, although he feels a fool for doing so. Why offer an apology for prolonging someone's life? He tells her that as soon as he knows further details he will advise her immediately. She looks at him blankly, which he takes as a sign that she is done with him and he escapes back to completing his report.

9:50AM 18ᵗʰ May 1536

The Lodgings of the Lieutenant of the Tower

50 minutes after the scheduled time of Anne Boleyn's execution

The swordsman is giving Walsingham his views on the delay. They aren't particularly positive.

Such things are better done quickly, he presses.

Why isn't a new time for the execution scheduled? He demands.

He is a professional doing a job. He wants to be treated like one. Preparation is key, he cannot be expected to throw it all together at the last moment as though it didn't matter.

Delays would make the lady more agitated. An agitated prisoner means more room for error, he repeated. He was sure that the constable and the king wanted no errors.

Walsingham could give the man no answers.

The swordsman, like everyone else, would have to wait.

10:02AM 18ᵗʰ May 1536

The residence of the Imperial Ambassador

Just over one hour after the scheduled time of Anne Boleyn's execution

Chapuys' man is rushed into his master's bedroom. Chapuys ignores the latest wave of pain from the gout and immediately demands to know if the job is done. His man explains that at almost fifteen minutes past the scheduled hour he and others before him had been removed from the Tower. He explains that he believed that all foreigners were being expelled, though for what reason he does not know.

He does not know when the execution would take place.

He also explains that he had paid a bookseller that he knew to go to the tower and watch. If there was news, the bookseller would immediately come here and report. It would cost a further five pounds, but Chapuys' man believes it will be worth the expense.

Chapuys knows that he will receive reports from Lady Kingston at some point. He also has a network of other contacts throughout the city and within Whitehall. When something is known he will receive news.

Until then, all he can do is wait.

What had happened? Was there a last minute reprieve? Had the concubine agreed that her marriage was false all along and to go to a nunnery? Of course, with Cromwell's closure of the religious houses he was not sure where that would be. A thousand questions run through his mind.

But for the answers Chapuys will have to wait like everyone else.

10:15 AM 18ᵗʰ May 1536

Greenwich Palace, London.

1 hour and 15 minutes after the scheduled time of Anne Boleyn's execution

The Princess Elizabeth is looking out of the widow towards the waters of the Thames.

The boats pass up and down going about their business.

Slowly Elizabeth raises her finger and points down the river towards the Tower.

"When will I see Mother?" she asks quietly.

Everyone else in the room freezes in horror at the question. The fact that the three-year-old child is staring down the river towards where her mother is facing her death and asking about seeing her was unnerving to say the least. All eyes turn to Lady Bryan, Elizabeth's governess.

Lady Bryan knows perfectly well that the pointed finger towards the Tower does not relate to the question. Elizabeth is unaware of anything untoward occurring at the Tower. She couldn't possibly know where her mother is or the fate awaiting her.

"Soon," Lady Bryan quickly lies. "Shall we go and play with your dolls?"

10:35AM 18ᵗʰ May 1536

The residence of the Imperial Ambassador

1 hour and 35 minutes after the scheduled time of Anne Boleyn's execution

A short note arrives from Lady Kingston.

It tells Chapuys that the execution has been delayed until at least noon in order that all strangers might be removed from within the walls of the Tower.

Chapuys breathes a sigh of relief. There was no reprieve. The concubine was still going to her death, albeit it on unjust charges. However, at least the king had not taken her back.

He decides he needs to get more eyes within the Tower to witness the events when they occur. He knows from experience that one man's report on an event could be very different from another. The more eyes, the better.

He calls his man and they decide which of the numerous Englishmen in their pay to send.

10:50AM 18ᵗʰ May 1536

The Residence of Thomas Cromwell

1 hour and 50 minutes after the scheduled time of Anne Boleyn's execution

Cromwell receives Kingston's extraordinary report regarding the events of the morning.

As well as his details of being present at the queen's last confession and her lack of admission of guilt, Kingston highlights some thoughts.

He says that the strangers are expelled from the Tower, although there were less than thirty in number when all was done.

Secondly, he suggests that if the execution were to proceed today then there were likely to be few witnesses. Kingston's view is that sufficient independent witnesses are essential so that news may be spread that the queen had been delivered by the king's justice in a manner befitting her station.

Cromwell knows there is a fine line they must tread.

The job needed to done and done quickly. The king demanded it. Until it was done Cromwell was still fearful of a Boleyn faction resurgence, no matter how unlikely. And yet it had to be done well. The king had cast aside one queen that was beloved by the people for this lady. Despite her general unpopularity, Cromwell was aware that there was a growing voice on the streets that the lady had not been tried fairly. The last thing that was needed was for the king's reputation to suffer again through this.

With enough witnesses to the execution, word would naturally spread that it had been done well. With enough time, the guilds could send representatives to the Tower. They were respected men, the people would listen and believe what they said. With enough time, those at court who wished to attend would be able. The presence of high ranking individuals would add to credibility. Given sufficient time, there would be enough talk made around London that the common man could attend as well if he wished.

Kingston was right.

A further delay was needed.

With reluctance Cromwell composed a message to Kingston informing him that the execution should be put back until nine of the clock the next day. The ban on strangers still stood, but the gates should remain open to Englishmen and women. He told Kingston that he would be there himself just before the appointed hour.

Following the message to Kingston, he wrote to the Lord Mayor instructing him to attend the Tower on the morrow with the aldermen of the city. He was also to arrange the attendance of representatives of the various guilds. Cromwell offered praise on how the Mayor could be trusted to handle this important task. However, written between the flowery praise were sinister threats. The Lord Mayor would know that this was a task that must not be fouled up.

After the messages were dispatched, Cromwell set out for Whitehall.

The king must be informed of proceedings and Cromwell isn't looking forward to it at all.

10:55AM 18ᵗʰ May 1536

Sir William Paulet's house, Chelsea

Almost two hours after the scheduled time of Anne Boleyn's execution

A messenger arrives from Whitehall Palace. A messenger from the king himself.

There is a note for Sir John Seymour and a package for his daughter, Jane.

The Seymours had been lodging at Sir William's house over the past four days. The home had once been the property of Sir Thomas More and the king considered it suitable enough as lodgings for Jane and her family while events played themselves out at the Tower.

Sir John opens the message with a touch of excitement. He shouts out to his son, Edward, who had just heard the messenger's arrival.

"The king will be dining here tonight. He desires us all to be in attendance," relays Sir John.

Edward Seymour nods as though such messages arrive on a daily basis. He immediately begins to wonder what they should serve. He also wonders why he is yet to hear the cannon fire from the Tower. He calculates every possibility in his mind. Had the lady managed to get a letter to the king and he had been bent to her will once more? But no, if that were the case then he would not be attending here that evening. Was the deed done, yet for some unknown reason no cannon had sounded? He didn't know and he certainly wasn't going to ask this boy regarding such matters. His own man was at the Tower. He would report back soon enough. He could do nothing but wait.

"There is a package for Jane. Could you call her?" Sir John adds.

"No need, Father. I am here," says Jane entering the room. She is dressed in brilliant blue and moves with gentle grace. She is already starting to act like a queen.

"His Majesty sends you this, my Lady," the boy says, holding out the velvet bag.

Jane looks excited. Henry was a most generous suitor. He was always sending her gifts of jewels, furs or new clothes. Like any young woman, Jane loved receiving expensive gifts.

She opens up the bag and draws out a string of the most beautiful pearls she had ever seen. She holds them in her hands, running them through her fingers, admiring their beauty.

But she feels something strange as she looked at the gift. She also feels horror.

"Jane," comes the sharp interruption of her father. "You have a message to give to the king?"

Jane recovers her manners, "Tell his Majesty that he is too generous to a poor girl like me. I could never repay him."

The messenger nods.

"And tell his Majesty that we are honoured that he would grace us with his presence this evening," adds Sir John. "Honoured beyond measure, is that not so, Edward?"

Edward Seymour isn't listening; he is watching his sister intently.

The boy doesn't wait for him to add anything, he simply bows and leaves to relay the messages to the king. He knows that Henry would be especially eager to hear what Mistress Seymour had thought of his gift.

After the messenger leaves Edward approaches Jane who is still staring at the pearls. "What is it?"

"These," she says, looking up at him with fear in her eyes "Look at them! Who do they remind you of?"

Edward Seymour stares back blankly.

"Her! The necklace she always used to wear, the one with the letter B hanging from it."

"What of it?"

"What if I don't please him? What if I don't give him what he wants? It could be me in the Tower," whispers Jane, her hands trembling.

"Then give him what he wants, dear sister," hisses back Edward. "This family's prosperity depends upon it."

11:15 AM 18th May 1536

Hunsdon House - Hunsdon, Hertfordshire

Two and a quarter hours after the scheduled time of Anne Boleyn's execution

The Lady Mary has just received her third important message of the morning.

She has already received a letter from Lady Carew and a brief message from Chapuys. Now it is a letter from Lady Kingston.

All told her, in slightly different ways, the same thing.

That morning her enemy would be dead.

Mary could not quite believe it. For years the name of Anne Boleyn had brought grief to her heart. First the she-devil had bewitched and corrupted her father, causing him to cast aside his true wife, her loyal mother. Then, she had caused him to curse his eternal soul and the spiritual wellbeing of his people by also casting aside Rome and the Holy Father. When Mary had refused to accept what the lady had made him do, then she too was humiliated: demoted from a princess to nothing, an inconsequential mistake of her father. Not only that, but she was made to serve upon her father's bastard daughter, Elizabeth. Her, his true and legitimate daughter, the heir to his realm, a princess not only of England but of Spain as well, had been made to serve on the child of a whore. Of course, she wasn't her father's heir any longer. The she-devil had made her father declare her a bastard and remove all of her rights to the succession. Parliament played along to the woman's tune. Then, Mary had suffered the ultimate grief. The whore had managed to poison her beloved mother as she had always vowed. The poison she administered was so fearful that it turned her mother's heart pure black and stopped its beating. There were constant fears that she herself would suffer the same fate. Mary knew that the witch would do it if she could. Her friends at court had said the woman spoke about it often enough. So real were the fears around her supporters that Chapuys had even arranged her transport out of the country to the safety of Spain. But Mary knew that if she left she would never return and all of the claims that were rightfully hers would be lost forever. She did what her mother would have done. She stayed to fight.

After the swordsman at the Tower had done his work there would no more fears of poisoning.

Mary had been receiving regular reports of Anne's downfall. She had many loyal supporters at her father's court and many of them had the courage to inform her of events in London. Of course, none were more loyal than Chapuys who had kept up a constant stream of communication. She had been hearing stories for over a month on how the whore had fallen from her father's favour. Even before then, she rejoiced on hearing the news that she had miscarried a son. There were stories from Chapuys of his secret meetings with Cromwell in which they discussed her restoration to the succession and of new alliances with Spain. Yet the messages ebbed and flowed like the tides. After a period of positive news, then came a set back with news of an argument between her father and Chapuys and the fact that Cromwell had overstepped the mark. She had been incensed to read that

Chapuys had even acknowledged the lady in chapel, something that he had always sworn not to do.

The reports from the trial were scandalous, but hardly surprising in Mary's eyes. She could not help but wonder if the child Elizabeth, whom she had actually grown quite fond of despite matters, was actually her father's daughter at all. The more she thought of it, the more she convinced herself that she was not. As she read through the names of the guilty men she grew more and more appalled. Smeaton? A mere court musician? What sexual desires must the woman have to lower herself to a musician? Her own brother? Did her depravity know no bounds? Was she that desperate for a son to secure her place that she would break God's holy laws?

As she read Lady Kingston's letter, she knew that even as she read, the lady could be dead. But she assumed nothing. Her father's mind changed like the wind. She would save her rejoicing for the news to be confirmed. All who wrote to her promised her the news from the Tower at the earliest opportunity.

She could only wait.

But she couldn't help but wonder of her own position. She wondered as to the inclinations of Mistress Seymour whom Chapuys believed her father would now take as his wife. Would she have a new enemy or a new unexpected friend?

Time would tell.

12:02PM 18ᵗʰ May 1536

The Constables' Lodgings, The Tower of London.

Just less than twenty-one hours until Anne Boleyn's execution

Ralph Sadler arrives with his message from Cromwell.

Kingston reads it and agrees with the decision, despite the fact he would rather not have to care for the prisoner for another day.

Sadler leaves to meet Cromwell at Whitehall.

Kingston informs Walsingham of the new orders and they agree to meet in one hour to discuss arrangements.

Kingston brushes himself off and steadies himself for a difficult conversation. He decides he might visit the privy first.

12:07PM 18ᵗʰ May 1536

The king's privy apartments, Whitehall

Twenty hours and 53 minutes until Anne Boleyn's execution

Thomas Cromwell's meeting with the king is brief.

"Is it done?" the king demands. "There was no cannon?"

"Majesty, I regret it has become necessary to postpone till the morrow. There were many arrangements to make and time was not in our favour. I'm sure that your Majesty will agree that the matter should be handled well." Cromwell replies, hopeful that the king will see matters the same way.

Henry remains quiet for a while and Cromwell braces himself for a rebuke. Instead, the king seems very calm, "I just want it done, Cromwell."

"I understand, your Majesty," replies Cromwell. "But I am considering how it will look to your subjects."

"My subjects are just that, Cromwell. I am their king," spits back Henry, determined not to be dictated to by the will of his subjects. He is king and his will must be obeyed at all times, their uneducated opinions do not matter.

"Of course, but there are also the various ambassadors to consider. They will all be sending reports to their masters. All must be done according to the law and correct procedure," offers Cromwell in return. It was a game that he played with king on a regular basis: agree with all that was said but offer a different course of action.

Once again Henry is silent. Cromwell is right. The man had made the correct call and that is why he was Henry's man. Henry congratulates himself on the appointment of a capable and able minister. Procedure and appearance were far more important than speed, Henry would have said the very same thing. "Agreed. Yet there can be no more delays. I have been publicly wronged and the matter must be concluded to my satisfaction."

"Yes, your Majesty."

Henry waves his hand in a dismissive manner.

Cromwell bows and makes his exit.

"Cromwell!" Henry suddenly booms.

Cromwell's heart is in his mouth. The king must have thought of a reason to be offended, or encountered a problem in his mind. He turns to face his king's wrath.

Henry's voice drops so it is barely a whisper, "I want to hear the cannon when it is done; I want to rejoice. And I want no communication from her. If a letter is sent, then burn it. Understand?"

"Majesty," Cromwell confirms with a nod of his head and rushes off. He still has a busy day ahead of him.

12:17PM 18th May 1536

The Queen's Lodgings - The Tower of London

Twenty hours and 43 minutes until Anne Boleyn's execution

Sir William Kingston enters the Queen's Lodgings and informs Anne Boleyn that the execution has been postponed until the following morning at nine of the clock.

The news is first greeted with anger by Anne. Then woeful desperation.

She begs Kingston to speak to the king to allow her to die that afternoon. She tells him that she does not wish for death, but has resolved herself to die and she wishes to be dispatched without delay. She tells him she fears that delay will weaken her resolve.

Kingston fully understands Anne's position. He has seen enough prisoners in their final hours to know that awaiting death was a torment to the mind. The woman had summoned up the resolve to face the swordsman once. Now she has to repeat the process. Again he prays that her mind would hold out till the morrow. The manic laughter and the jest about her neck had told him that she was close to the edge. He would get his wife to speak to Lady Boleyn. It is imperative that Anne be kept calm.

Kingston leaves telling Lady Boleyn that they would dine as normal.

12:45PM 18ᵗʰ May 1536

The Residence of the Lord Mayor of London

Twenty hours and 15 minutes until Anne Boleyn's execution

Sir John Aleyn, Lord Mayor of London, physically shivers as he reads the message from Cromwell.

It is true. The king is about to do the unthinkable and execute his queen. It seems that there would be no reprieve. It will happen on the morrow at nine of the clock. It is a terrible thing which he could hardly comprehend.

To make matters worse, he is being dragged into it.

Sir John runs his fingers through what remained of his hair as he reads the message a second time. Being present at the event himself is no problem, although the thought of witnessing it does not fill him with joy. No, the problem he has is the need to assemble those whom Cromwell has demanded. Many members of the guilds are sympathetic to the queen's cause. The question he has is who would be willing to attend? What would happen if he could not summon the numbers demanded in the communication?

Time is short.

He begins writing.

There is much to do.

1:22PM 18ᵗʰ May 1536

The Constables' Lodgings, The Tower of London.

Nineteen hours and 38 minutes until Anne Boleyn's execution

Kingston and Walsingham look at each other with resignation on their faces. They have formulated their plans and now know that they have a long day of preparation ahead of them. Both men know that this is the way it should have been handled in the first place. Kingston in particular feels slightly ashamed that just a few hours ago he was preparing to supervise the execution of the Queen of England without the necessary pomp and procedure.

Now matters will be corrected.

The lady would be treated with the utmost respect.

The king would suffer no shame.

And Kingston would receive no rebukes.

Hopefully.

1:45PM 18th May 1536

The Lodgings of the Lieutenant of the Tower

Nineteen hours and 15 minutes until the time of Anne Boleyn's execution

The swordsman looks disgusted at being made to wait.

"Sir, I had expected to be on my way home by now," he complains again.

Walsingham keeps his cool. He knows that the man had been personally hired by Cromwell. Despite desiring to dismiss him and replace him with the executioner of the Tower, he nods his head as though he agrees.

"This is as my Lord Cromwell desires," explains Walsingham. "The king desires it too. And you are being compensated well for the task, are you not?"

The swordsman lets out a low groan that may have confirmed his agreement.

"Until the morrow my hospitality is at your disposal." Walsingham gives a sweeping gesture to indicate that the swordsman can do as he pleases. He would have preferred suggesting the swordsman take in the pleasures, dubious or otherwise, of the city. However, he and Kingston had discussed the need to ensure the swordsman remained in the Tower. It would not be good if the executioner forgot himself at some house in Southwark and failed to return at the appointed hour.

"I thank you, sir," the swordsman replies, accepting that this is how it is. He removes his blade from its scabbard and begins lightly oiling it with a well-used cloth.

Walsingham looks at the blade glinting in the light and the beautiful and graceful face of the queen fills his mind. He cannot believe what his king has ordered him to do.

1:55PM 18ᵗʰ May 1536

Whitehall Palace

Nineteen hours and 5 minutes until Anne Boleyn's execution

The arrow buries itself into the target a little less than 4 inches from the bull.

A murmur of appreciation rumbles through the handful of men present.

"I may as well give up now, Harry," declares Suffolk with a grin on his face.

Henry turns to his opponent with a little swagger, "I presumed you already had, Charles."

Everyone laughs at the king's gentle mocking of his friend. However, the king had actually got it spot on. Suffolk had no intention of darkening the king's mood today, he assured the majority of his arrows were a little off line. He did fire the occasional good shot; Henry was pretty astute at determining when people weren't trying when competing against him. At cards, even if Henry found it annoying, he at least got their coin at the end of the evening, but at sport it brought him no joy. Henry wanted to play the best and beat the best. Today he wants to blow off some steam. He rather fancies a game of tennis, but his legs are still not the same after his jousting accident earlier that year. If he can't compete at his best, then he isn't going to compete at all. Today, archery will have to do.

Suffolk was still his greatest rival. Regretfully, Bryan was no archer, not with his one eye. His son, Richmond, was getting better, but was still no competition for his father. Many of his Yeoman guard could have given him a match, but the vast majority would not have the courage to beat him.

Henry turns back to the target and raises the bow. Slowly and steadily he draws back on the string and after a moment's hesitation he lets fly. The arrow buries itself into the middle of the bull.

The king accepts the applause from those assembled, with a grin.

He hasn't thought about his prisoner in the Tower since the minute Cromwell had left.

2:05PM 18ᵗʰ May 1536

The Constables' Lodgings, The Tower of London.

Eighteen hours and 55 minutes until the time of Anne Boleyn's execution

The queen is a changed woman.

Barely an hour and a half ago she had been begging to die, now there is no mention of death whatsoever. She doesn't go so far as to mention a reprieve, but Kingston senses a new optimism about her. However, he also knows that she can change demeanour in a heartbeat.

She eats little. In fairness, Kingston had hardly ever seen her eat well even when she was presiding over great feasts in court at the king's side. Kingston doubts he could eat a thing if he were in her position.

Her talk is of religion and the interpretation of the Bible. On more than one occasion his wife gives him a look that seems to suggest she believes the queen's words are nothing short of heresy. Kingston would listen politely if it kept her calm, and let her talk however much heresy she desires.

He is glad that this is the last such meal he will have to endure.

As long as there are no further alterations to the orders.

3:00PM 18ᵗʰ May 1536

The Queen's Apartments, The Tower of London

Eighteen hours until Anne Boleyn's execution

The queen has summoned Lady Kingston to her apartments. She has taken her alone into the presence chamber and has locked the door.

"Pray be seated, Madam," says Anne, pointing to the chair of estate that dominates the room.

Lady Kingston looks aghast, "It is my duty to stand in your presence. Much less that I sit upon the seat of state belonging to you, the queen."

"Come, Madam," replies Anne wryly, "I am queen no longer. I am a condemned person and by law I have nothing left in this world. All that remains is for me to clear my conscience. Pray be seated."

"I have often played the fool in my youth and to fulfil your command I will do it once more in my advanced age," agrees Lady Kingston and sits down upon the great chair of estate and waits for Anne to speak.

The queen then does something that Lady Kingston was not expecting. She throws herself to her knees and allows the tears to flow down her cheeks.

"I know that you are friends well with the Lady Mary, the king's daughter," begins Anne. "My conscience cannot be quiet at this time. I am down on my knees before you as I would if the Lady Mary were here herself. I should desire that you request of the Lady her forgiveness for all of the terrible wrongs that I have placed upon her in her life."

Lady Kingston is unsure of how to respond. There is no doubt that the woman on her knees in tears has treated the Lady Mary terribly over many years. The fact that she encouraged the king not to permit Mary to visit her mother in her final days was nothing short of inhumane. She has no love or fondness for the woman, and thinks that the king has finally done well to put her back in her place.

However, before Lady Kingston can think of a reply the queen speaks again, this time her voice no more than a whisper.

"I beg of you to fulfil this request directly to the Lady Mary in person. And I pray that you do not divulge this conversation with any person other than the lady herself. I should wish it be the case that she receive these words as directly from my lips as it is possible, without twisting and shaping from other persons."

Lady Kingston isn't shocked that Anne is aware that she has been reporting every word to different parties: she knows the queen has considerable wit. She is, however a little taken aback with how earnest her desire seems to be for her to pass on this message.

Again, Anne speaks before Lady Kingston can consider the request. "You speak not Madam and I understand why. I hath not been a good mistress to the Lady in question. For my actions against her truly I deserve to die. Tomorrow I will do just that. Yet the lady must know how sorry I am for my harshness towards her. Like my own sweet child, she is the king's own daughter and for that I should have shown her kindness. I have failed terribly in that one duty. I beg of you to carry this message unto her. And pray that you do not whisper a word of it to your husband or other persons."

The sight of the queen on her knees with the tears flooding down her face moves Lady Kingston. Despite her better judgement she finds herself agreeing to the request.

3:15PM 18th May 1536

The residence of Thomas Cromwell

Seventeen hours and 45 minutes until Anne Boleyn's execution

"The king is leaving the palace this evening," Cromwell had told Ralph Sadler. "Once he is gone, that is the time to complete this task."

Sadler has in his hand Cromwell's orders to remove all portraits of Anne Boleyn from Whitehall. Cromwell has spent the last half hour issuing orders for all of the king's major palaces to do the same. They would be dispatched shortly. However, Cromwell wishes to ensure that the palace in which the king is currently residing is cleansed of her image first. He will entrust Ralph to oversee the task so that, when the king returns from visiting Mistress Seymour, he won't be haunted by the image of the queen he is about to execute. Wriothesley would then produce copies of the orders for all Henry's minor residences and hunting lodges. They could be dispatched over the next few days as it was unlikely that the king would be visiting any in the immediate days ahead.

"And they are to be replaced with what?" Ralph asks.

"Anything," insists Cromwell. "I believe there are portraits of the king's mother that could be moved to these more prominent positions. I will leave it to your judgement."

Ralph nods and leaves so that the work can begin as soon as Henry leaves Whitehall.

Cromwell then starts work writing letters commissioning stonemasons and painters. All the queen's devices and symbols will have to be obliterated over the coming weeks. Mistress Seymour had her own device of a phoenix emerging from a burning castle. The phoenix would soon be replacing the falcons that had only just finished replacing the pomegranate.

He knew one thing… it was all going to cost a fortune.

3:30PM 18ᵗʰ May 1536

The Constables' Lodgings, The Tower of London.

Seventeen and a half hours until Anne Boleyn's execution

Kingston awakes with a start, sweat pouring down his spine.

He has been dozing in his chair. Since this whole saga began he has slept little. After the events of the morning he had decided he would sit and read some correspondence unrelated to the execution of the queen. But after a hearty meal and an extra mug of ale, sleep had overwhelmed him.

He rather wishes it hadn't. He had a terrible nightmare. The queen had been missing from her rooms when he went to collect her for her execution. He blamed the guards. Cromwell blamed him. The King blamed everyone. And it was he, not the queen, who climbed the steps of the scaffold to await the cold, steel blade of the hangman of Calais. He was saying his final prayers when he had awoken.

Clearly the pressure of recent weeks was beginning to get to him.

The amount of work and responsibility assigned to him was of the level that would break lesser men.

Four men of the royal court, incarcerated under his guard, had been tried at Westminster Hall and condemned to death. Then they were executed publicly on the hill and buried. One peer of the realm, likewise. Two more men of court imprisoned in the Bell and Byward towers – of their fate he knew nothing; he simply had to keep them alive. There were regular visits from Cromwell as well as the daily reports. Also he made regular trips to visit the king at Whitehall and Hampton Court. He had a show trial to arrange, with the leading peers in attendance, with little more than twenty-four hours' notice. And then the none-too-small matter of the imprisonment, trial and execution of the Queen of England.

As soon as the trial was ordered Kingston had had no doubt of the verdict which would be returned. As Cardinal Wolsey had once told him, "If the crown were prosecutor and asserted it, justice would be found to bring in a verdict that Abel was the murderer of Cain."

These were ludicrous times. But he wasn't broken yet.

All his prisoners had made their own demands of Kingston in different ways. Many of these matters appeared to be trifling to Kingston in view of what awaited them, but for the prisoners they meant much.

For example, Lord Rochford, the queen's brother, was full of concern about the Abbot of Valle Crucis Abbey. He wanted to be sure that, as the abbey was being suppressed, the Abbot would not lose his pension. He also expressed similar concerns regarding the finances of the Bishop of Dublin. He insisted that Kingston write to Cromwell about the matter, pressing him to urge the king to remember his duty, especially to the Abbot.

Weston had taken the time and had the memory to sit down and make a full list of his debts, which began with two amounts to the king but also included sums to Cornelius Heyss, the king's goldsmith. Hannesley's poor wife also required payment for four tennis balls. When he summed up the total it came to a mighty £925.7s.2d. As well as the list of debts, he also wrote a touching letter to his parents. Both of these documents were entrusted to Kingston for delivery post mortem.

The organisation of the various events and the passing of orders had not been straightforward. Not only were there the current issues with the execution of the queen, but there had also been grave uncertainties of the executions of the five convicted men. Until the morning of their execution the order had not been received to commute the sentence from the traditional traitor's death of being hanged, drawn, dismembered and quartered at Tyburn, to the more merciful end of decapitation with the axe. Kingston could almost feel the pain of the men as they agonised, waiting for this news. At least now their deaths were swift.

The queen's death would be swifter still. The executioner of Calais was known throughout Europe for his skill, and it was a further act of compassion on the king's part to grant it.

Kingston simply prayed that the queen would be within her apartments when he went to collect her in the morning.

He arises from his chair and wipes his face with a wet cloth to expel the last traces of sleep. He knows there will be enough time for rest once this is over.

4:00 PM 18ᵗʰ May 1536

The Bell Tower, The Tower of London

Seventeen hours until Anne Boleyn's execution

Sir Richard Page wallows in his undershirt in his room. He is unshaven and has been since he heard of the guilty verdicts against the five men. His plate of food remains untouched. Over the last week he has lost weight significantly.

He is a wreck. A shell of the man he was before. Why? Because he is the forgotten man.

Wyatt had received word from Cromwell that he would face no further action. Wyatt had to trust that this would be the case, yet at least he had received word. Page had received no such word and yet, despite his own arrest on the 5ᵗʰ of May, he had not been sent to trial. He was captain of the king's own bodyguard and vice-chamberlain to his bastard son Richmond. Page wondered how the king could question his loyalty after all of these years. Yet, clearly he did.

He prays that his family connections to Fitzwilliam will save him. Surely if he were to be executed he would have been sent to trial with the others?

Torment fills his mind.

He looks at the uneaten apple on his plate and feels nauseous.

The only thing he can do is wait.

And pray.

5:00PM 18ᵗʰ May 1536

Lambeth Palace

Sixteen hours until Anne Boleyn's execution

Word finally reaches Archbishop Cranmer that there has been a delay in the execution till the morrow.

He feels conflicting emotions. Firstly, elation that the queen still lives, swiftly followed by pain that, come evening tomorrow, she will not.

However, Cranmer has been close enough to Henry to know how his mood and mind can change with the wind. He knows that while the queen lived, there is still hope. It is that hope that he clutches to now. He considers again writing to the king, making a plea on the queen's behalf. But once again he decides against it. Despite his grief, he does not wish to fall alongside his patron.

He reflects on what he sees as cowardliness.

Yet he knows that the king's will shall be done. If this course of action were his chosen path, then it would come to pass no matter what Cranmer pleaded.

Instead, he sends word to the Tower to enquire as to whether the queen will require him on the morrow.

5:03PM 18ᵗʰ May 1536

Whitehall Palace, London.

Less than sixteen hours until Anne Boleyn's execution

Henry VIII checks his appearance in the mirror and smooths down his beard. He points to his sleeve and his page makes some adjustments until the king grunts an approval.

Middle age is starting to catch up with Henry. His waist is starting to thicken. His hair is thinning and has silver flecks. His body, not helped by a devastating jousting accident not four months ago, simply can no longer do what it used to. It angers Henry, who still believes in his mind he is the strutting seventeen-year old who first came to the throne.

His personal vanity is greater than any person's within the court.

No one dares point out that he is getting old.

However, in rare moments of personal honesty he knows it. And, more importantly, he knows he has no legitimate heir.

Cromwell is currently working on a bill that will allow the king to name his own successor. Henry has it in his mind to name his bastard son Henry Fitzroy, Duke of Richmond and Somerset, as his heir. But the king is worried about Fitzroy's health. Fitzroy is trying to disguise it, but the king fears he has consumption. A legitimate heir would solve the issue of the succession once and for all.

The king makes a crude joke with Sir Francis Bryan who laughs heartily. The two walk together through the palace which is far quieter now the queen's household has been disbanded. There is a general fear around court. People wonder who will receive a knock on the door next. A few brave souls attempt to approach the king with petitions. He roars at Richard Rich to deal with them. Henry and Bryan continue through the rose gardens to the banks of the river, where they board the king's royal barge. Like all journeys Henry has made since becoming king, his personal lifeguards accompany him every step of the way.

Yesterday Cromwell had advised the king not to be seen in public at present. Despite Anne's widespread unpopularity amongst the general population there was a growing degree of sympathy for the woman in the Tower. A low profile would be best. Henry doesn't quite see it the same way. He is the one who has been wronged. He is the one who has been bewitched. He believes the five men who went to the scaffold yesterday morning were just a handful of those guilty. Henry now believes that Anne had more than one hundred men in her bed since their marriage. And now Cromwell advises him to keep to his palace? But Henry had seen how his subjects rallied in support of Katherine of Aragon, the Dowager Princess. He trusts that Cromwell knows the mood in London and decides to take his advice. However, this is a visit he has no intention of postponing.

He has a young maiden to romance.

A woman that he has already told Cromwell he will make his queen. She, in turn, will give him the heir that two women have already failed to provide.

The River Thames and the royal barge make it an easy journey.

Bryan had been promoting the cause of the Seymours for a while. He could see that his second cousin Anne Boleyn no longer had the king's favour. He has been working with the Seymour brothers recently to put Jane under the eye of the king. A new queen would mean new favour and new riches.

Francis Bryan is one of Henry's closest companions. Over the next few years he would grow closer still, especially since Henry Norris had lost his head just the day before. He lost an eye in a tournament some years ago and since then has been forced to wear a patch over the vacant socket. Somehow this makes him more appealing to the young women at court and his reputation doesn't put them off. He has been a willing participant in assisting Henry to conduct his extra marital activities, on more than one occasion advising the king from personal experience of the lady in question.

As he is rowed up the Thames, Henry feels the excitement of the chase in his stomach which causes him to feel once more like a seventeen-year-old.

5:15PM 18th May 1536

The Residence of Thomas Cromwell, London

Fifteen hours and 45 minutes until Anne Boleyn's execution

Thomas Cromwell is reading some of his recent correspondence.

Despite the tension that has been surrounding him recently, he cannot help but laugh. The vultures were circling.

There is a letter from Lord Lisle asking that Cromwell consider him when dividing up Norris's land and offices. The joke was that it had been dated after Norris's arrest yet before his sentence had been confirmed. These people had simply no shame. Yet he has to laugh at the man's audacity. It was the type of thing that he may have done in the past. Simply for his boldness he would remember Lisle when gifts were made.

6:00PM 18ᵗʰ May 1536

The Queen's Apartments, The Tower of London

Fifteen hours until Anne Boleyn's execution

Anne Boleyn has been less troubled since her meeting alone with Lady Kingston. She has been working alone on some poetry, the papers in front of her are full of scratches and corrections. But she has written out the completed verses on a fresh sheet.

O death! rock me asleep,
Bring me on quiet rest;
Yet pass my guiltless ghost
Out of my careful breast:
Toll on the passing bell,
Ring out the doleful knell,
Let the sound of my death tell,
For I must die,
There is no remedy,
For now I die
My pains who can express?
Alas! they are so strong,
My dolor will not suffer strength
My life for to prolong:
Toll on the passing bell, etc.
Alone, in prison strong,
I wail my destiny,
Wo worth this cruel hap that I
Should taste this misery:
Toll on the passing bell, etc.
Farewell my pleasures past,
Welcome my present pain;
I feel my torments so increase

That life cannot remain.
Cease now the passing bell,
Rung is my doleful knell,
For the sound my death doth tell,
Death doth draw nigh,
Sound my end dolefully,
For now I die.

She reads and smiles, as though she were still composing words and songs with her ladies in Greenwich. She calls over Margaret and entrusts her with the sheet of paper. She tells her that she must ensure that the piece is handed to someone appropriate.

Margaret agrees despite the fact she does not really know who to give it to.

7:25PM 18ᵗʰ May 1536

The Residence of Thomas Cromwell

Thirteen hours and 35 minutes until the execution of Anne Boleyn

Cromwell is pacing in his office while Thomas Wriothesley takes notes.

"Lord Warden of the Cinque Ports shall be Sir Thomas Cheyney," states Cromwell. He continues his pacing, but waits for Wriothesley to catch up. "The Duke of Richmond is to be granted Chamberlain of Chester and of North Wales. Mr Bryan is to be made Chief Gentleman of the King's Privy Chamber, upon the king's consent to the matter."

Cromwell returns to his desk to consult a written note on a sheet of paper. "Add a reminder to consider the mastership of Bedlam for Mr Robert Barnes. Also, something for Lord Lisle."

He then adds his own handwritten note to the sheet he was consulting. It simply says - Remember Sir William Kingston.

The task of dividing up the pie from the executed men has begun.

7:30PM 18th May 1536

The Seymour Residence, Chelsea

The king is holding court at table. He is at his charismatic best.

He is telling stories of his sole victory in battle, the Battle of the Spurs, so called as the French simply turned and fled. He does not mention that while he was seeing off a couple of hundred gutless Frenchmen, Queen Katherine was seeing off over twenty-thousand rampaging Scots who had poured in over the border at home.

Edward and Thomas Seymour in particular are lapping it up. John Seymour can hardly believe what is happening. Francis Bryan is smiling at every word Henry utters. And Jane sits at his right hand, eats little, and tries to have no opinion on anything at all.

This is hardly her first encounter with the king. He has been showing his interest in her for months now. They had been alone together, but other than some stolen kisses, sexual matters had not progressed further. She had been told by her brothers to keep Henry at arm's length. She must at all costs not visit his bed. Do this, they told her, and one day she would be a queen.

She could not deny that she was enthralled by Henry. Possibly she may say that she was in love. In this game of power that they were all playing it was hard to tell what it was that she actually felt.

She cared little for these set piece planned occasions that were all for show. It was the spontaneous happenings that she lived for, the moments alone where she could find the real Henry. Such as the time when she had sat on his knee and his hands were everywhere. Then of course the queen had walked in and there was a terrible argument. But it was exciting, the feeling of living for the moment. If her brothers hadn't instructed otherwise she knows she would have willingly visited Henry's bed.

Her brother Edward had told her it would not be much longer.

She is wearing the king's gift of pearls from earlier. The sudden touch of fear that she had felt after seeing them is gone. Edward was right, she had seen first-hand how her old mistress had lost the love of the king. Firstly, she had been too outspoken. Henry enjoyed intelligent conversation but he didn't tolerate being lectured, especially by his wife. Secondly, she had complained about his other women. Henry was the king; of course he was going to have women throw themselves at him. Finally, she had failed to provide the son he desired. When Jane provided the heir nothing else would matter. She would be untouchable.

She would be a queen. There would be feasts. Parties. Dancing. Women waiting on her. And there would be Henry's bed.

Jane wishes it would hurry up.

7:45 PM 18ᵗʰ May 1536

Hunsdon House, Hunsdon, Hertfordshire

Thirteen hours and 15 minutes until the execution of Anne Boleyn

It seemed that the Lady Mary would have to wait for her moment of triumph. Letters had been received from both Lady Kingston and Chapuys telling her of the delay at the Tower.

They both told her basically the same thing, probably because Chapuys had received his information from Lady Kingston in the first instance.

The execution was delayed until nine of the clock in the morning. There was no reason for concern, simply matters of formality and protocol.

Tomorrow would have to do, Mary thought.

Chapuys included a few interesting details in his message regarding Mistress Seymour. He believed more and more each day that she would be sympathetic to the Lady Mary's cause. Mary could only pray that this was true. The devil-woman had been making overtures of kindness over the last few months, but Mary was not to be blinded. She could never forgive the woman that had replaced and killed her mother. Mary wondered where Jane Seymour's heart lay in terms of religion. Might she encourage her father back to Rome and to stop the closure of the monasteries? She could only hope.

7:50 18ᵗʰ May 1536

The Queen's Apartments, The Tower of London

Thirteen hours and 10 minutes until the execution of Anne Boleyn

Anne Boleyn is shaking her head as her ladies hold up various gowns, underskirts, ropes and capes. Now that her poem was complete she was glad of something to pass the time.

She remembers the times when new gowns would arrive at the royal palaces. She would try them on and dance with her own reflection in the looking glass as her ladies fawned and leapt to her every pleasure.

Lady Boleyn sits in the corner sewing a piece of embroidery, she is not taking part in this folly. However, she is listening to every word, determined that if something of significance is spoken she will pass word on to Kingston.

Anne is fully aware that she isn't selecting gowns to wear to a dance or even to pack to take with her on progress. She is selecting what she will wear to die.

She is determined that she will leave making an unspoken statement.

8:00PM 18th May 1536

The residence of Thomas Cromwell

Thirteen hours until the execution of Anne Boleyn
Richard Cromwell brings his uncle reports from the streets of London.

It is as Thomas Cromwell suspected. Many people did not concern themselves with the downfall of the queen, they accepted it. However, a growing group was whispering that the queen was wrongly convicted. They said the king simply wanted rid of her and the peers had said guilty to please him.

And then there was something else. Richard hands him a scribbled note.

On it are the words of a ballad being sung about Mistress Seymour in some of the taverns that supported the queen.

The words are not complimentary.

Little could be done. Once tomorrow was over the king would remarry, and eventually London and the country would accept Jane as their queen.

8:35PM 18ᵗʰ May 1536

Rochford Hall, Essex

Twelve hours and 25 minutes until Anne Boleyn's execution

Mary Stafford, Boleyn that once was, can scarcely believe the note she has just received.

It told her that her brother George was dead and that by the time she read the letter, her sister the queen would likely have met the same fate. She is struggling to comprehend the rest of the message. Anne was convicted of high treason and had committed adultery with many men. George among them. Incest. Her siblings had committed incest and now they would die for it.

How in the name of God had this happened?

Out at Rockford Hall miles away from London, the court, and her sister, she was the forgotten Boleyn. When she chose to marry William Stafford her family disowned her. They let her live in near poverty, appalled at the fact that she had married for love. She had to appeal to Cromwell to intercede with her sister and the king. Of course Henry had discarded her many years ago, this was to be expected, but her own family? Even now the message informing her of her family's fate had not come from her mother or father, but a minor lady in waiting to her sister, who thought fit to tell her about the momentous events back in London.

Mary's eyes fell on the dresser and the large golden cup that adorned it. It had been a reconciliatory gift from her sister just a few months ago. With it came a purse of monies and the summons for young Katherine to attend court to act as a maid to her aunt. But there had been no suggestion of any return to court for Mary. In fact, there had been little correspondence after then. Now it seemed there would never be such a letter and there could never be a return.

In all honesty, Mary isn't sure how she feels. Certainly for a long time she had felt nothing for the family that had humiliated and discarded her. But now?

Her mind immediately leaps to her daughter. The letter had told her that Katherine was serving on Anne in the Tower. It is no place for a girl of her tender years. Mary wants her home. She thinks of writing to Cromwell to find out what had happened and to request that her daughter be returned to her. Cromwell had always had a favourable outlook towards her, some had whispered a few years earlier that he had looked to have her himself. Yet, something stops her.

The name Boleyn clearly mean nothing anymore; it is probably best that she stay here out of the way while Henry did his culling.

It is best to stay forgotten.

10:00PM 18ᵗʰ May 1536

Lambeth Palace

Eleven hours until Anne Boleyn's execution

Thomas Cranmer receives word from Kingston that the queen has spared him a repeat of yesterday.

He feels guilty that his immediate reaction is that of relief.

He has no desire to repeat the emotional process of yesterday, and is glad that the message says one of the queen's own chaplains would take Mass in the morning. He knows that in Anne's mind his principal task is over: he has heard her final confession in the presence of Kingston. She is aware that Kingston, and probably Cranmer himself, will have reported that confession to Cromwell by now, possibly even to the king. They will know that she said nothing that implied her guilt.

Like most of the senior members of court, Cranmer is drained. He knows he needs sleep. Yet he can't help but feel that he should have done more. He thinks on Saint Peter and his thrice denial of Christ before his crucifixion. Was his failure to press Anne's case with the king a denial? Was his relief at not being required at the Tower a denial? Would he deny Anne a third time?

He rushes off to his private chapel.

He needs to speak to God.

11:15PM 18ᵗʰ May 1536

The Queen's Lodgings, The Tower of London.

Nine hours and 45 minutes until Anne Boleyn's execution

Katherine Carey is asleep on a pallet.

Anne Boleyn looks at her with longing. Her niece has the rest of her life ahead of her. Not for the first time, she studies the girl and muses whether she is Henry's daughter. Mary wasn't sure. It was all so long ago and it doesn't matter now.

Anne wishes that she could sleep but she knows it will be a long, long night for her.

Margaret and Mary sit together working on embroidery and talking softly in hushed tones. They are as exhausted as Anne, but have vowed that on this final night they will stay awake with her as she wishes.

Lady Boleyn is also awake; she sits away from the other ladies reading a Bible. In a few hours Lady Kingston would come and relieve her so that she might be afforded some sleep. Cromwell has deemed that one of them must be present at all times during these final hours.

Anne knows that Skip will return in the early hours of the morning and she will repeat the process of preparing her soul for salvation.

It is a process that she hoped she will not need to go through again.

11:55PM 18th May 1536

The River Thames, London

Just over nine hours until the execution of Anne Boleyn

Henry VIII is being rowed back to Whitehall after his dinner with the Seymours.

Like Bryan, who again is accompanying him, he has drunk a little too much wine. But the cool night air is clearing his head.

There were discussions of the wedding when he spent time alone with Jane after the meal. In her effortlessly gracious manner she said that as long as she could marry him the wedding could take place in even the lowliest church in London. He had assured her that this would not be the case. On the other hand, he did not desire a pomp filled show such as Arthur had when he married Katherine. Better to get it done quickly, then she could set about the task of producing heirs. He favoured Hampton Court for the wedding, but would pass the matter to Cromwell to arrange the necessities. Maybe Whitehall would do for ease? There were many matters to be undertaken. A household had to be created, namely ladies-in-waiting, musicians, fools and chaplains. A suitable wedding gift had to be arranged in order that his new queen would have an income. No doubt there would be a glut of available properties to be granted. The crown had just received a windfall of land, properties and coin these past few days. Again, Cromwell would advance the matter.

The thought of the windfall from the seized assets of those who had been condemned brings his thoughts to Anne.

Try as he might he cannot ignore them. He thinks of his folly in his chase of the woman. How she had managed to drive him wild with desire and how he would chase after her like a lost puppy. But that was long ago. More recently she had behaved as though she had a right to the station to which he had elevated her. She had acted as though she, and not him, were monarch of this land. It was all part of her bewitching. Soon she would be gone and he could forget her.

His eyes happen upon an interlocked H and A painted in the middle of an elaborate decorative piece on the barge. He realises that there were many of these symbols of love throughout his palaces. Her falcon badge makes a frequent appearance as well. Forgetting her would be harder than he thought with these constant visual reminders everywhere he went. Then he pictures the great stained glass window in the Chapel Royal in Hampton Court. The stained glass of Saint Anne. That too would have to go.

He makes a mental note that it will be one more matter for Cromwell to handle, not knowing that Cromwell is, as normal, one step ahead and the work has already been commissioned.

2.30AM 19ᵗʰ May 1536

The rented house of Alexander Ales, London.

Six and a half hours until the time of Anne Boleyn's execution

Alexander Ales sits bolt upright in bed, the sweat pouring from his body and his heart thumping in his chest.

This isn't the first nightmare he has suffered since his excommunication at Holyrood two years ago. But this dream is something new. Something more troubling.

The theologian has been locked away in his room with his books for a number of days. The rooms are suited to study, and the fact that Cromwell had managed to find him such lodgings is highly conducive to work. He has no idea what was happening in the world outside.

He can't shake the terrible image from his mind. When he shuts his eyes it is all he sees.

Despite the dead of night, he decides to relate his story to his friend. Maybe he can tell him what it means.

He rises from bed and makes his way down to the river. He hopes to find someone there at this hour who can row him to Lambeth Palace.

3:55AM 19ᵗʰ May 1536

Lambeth Palace, London

Just over five hours until Anne Boleyn's execution

Alexander Ales enters the garden of Lambeth Palace knowing there is likely to be someone on duty to allow him entrance.

He is surprised to find Archbishop Cranmer awake and already walking in the gardens.

Cranmer is equally shocked at seeing his friend at this ungodly hour and enquires what on earth he is doing here as the clock has not yet struck four.

Ales says that he has had a horrific dream and wishes to hear Cranmer's interpretation of it.

Cranmer is not keen on being a consultant on matters of dream interpretation, but he sees that his learned friend is agitated and allows Ales to explain his tale.

"I saw white and green and then the Queen's head, which had been cut from her body. And her neck I could see so plainly that I could count the very nerves, veins and arteries within in it," recounts Ales, feeling his heart start to quicken in his chest once again.

Cranmer remains silent as he muses on the matter.

"Do you not know what is to happen today?" Cranmer finally asks.

"I have been at home working on my book these last few weeks. I confess I am aware of nothing that is occurring in the world," says a confused Ales.

Cranmer looks up to the heavens and manages to say, "She who has been the Queen of England upon the Earth will today become a queen in Heaven."

He can speak no more on the matter and bursts into tears.

4:30 AM 19ᵗʰ May 1536

The Queen's Lodgings - The Tower of London

Four and a half hours until Anne Boleyn's execution

Anne Boleyn is hearing Mass and taking her final Sacrament. Unlike yesterday, Archbishop Cranmer is not in attendance.

She is resolved and ready to die.

She prays there will be no further delay except in the case of a reprieve.

5:00AM 19ᵗʰ May 1536

The residence of Thomas Cromwell, London

Four hours until Anne Boleyn's execution

Cromwell is heading to an early morning meeting of his men.

His nephew Richard, Ralph Sadler and Thomas Wriothesley are all in attendance. Also present is his son Gregory.

It is rare for such a formal gathering to take place, especially so early in the morning. But these are exceptional times.

Cromwell issues instructions to each in turn. Wriothesley will remain here to direct urgent messengers to the Tower should they arrive. Sadler he sends to Whitehall in case the king should have need of him. Richard and his son would accompany him to the Tower to witness the execution.

After this morning any danger to himself will be over. Other than the king he will be the ultimate power in the land. He is determined that everyone should know it.

They all sit down to eat, unsure when they may be able to do so again.

The Queen's Lodgings - The Tower of London

Two hours until Anne Boleyn's execution

Anne Boleyn is eating a little breakfast with her ladies. Bread, cheese and cold chicken.

After two days with little sleep she is weary. But she will be able to rest soon enough.

No one is eating very much and the majority of the food remains untouched.

As she picks at her final meal, Anne cannot help but think back to some of the great feasts she has presided over with the king. Feasts where course after course was presented to her on golden plates, accompanied by grand fanfare. She would take a sample and then pass the plate over to favoured personages. How often had she passed those plates over to Norris? Or Weston? Or Brereton? Even her brother? Many times, too many to consider. But they weren't the only men. Who else had she favoured? Her father. Her uncle. Suffolk... although it had often pained her to do so. Cranmer. Cromwell. Yet they aren't here in the Tower. They weren't buried in the chapel without their heads. Why the lies?

Thomas Cromwell.

It is his name that keeps leaping to mind. Once he had been her great ally. He had finally managed to engineer Henry's annulment from Katherine of Aragon, putting right the mistakes the fool Wolsey had made before him. With the annulment secured she could finally become queen. Cromwell was her champion then. But in recent times she had become bitter towards him, resentful of the influence that he enjoyed with the king. Influence that once, not that long past, she had enjoyed. Maybe she had made an enemy of the wrong man?

She takes a bite of bread but it seems to stick in her dry throat. She remembers Henry's threat that he was the one who raised her up and he was the one that could take her down again. He had done just that. She knows she will not sit at the head of any great table hereafter. The dull Seymour girl would do that in her place. She would need to take care as to who she passed plates to and who she made enemies of. Because if she failed to give Henry a son then another foolish pretty girl would take her place.

"Eat, Katherine," Anne tells her niece as she watches the girl pick at her plate. "You need your strength."

Katherine tries a little more cheese but cannot stomach it. Anne does not reproach her again.
"I will dress now," Anne suddenly declares, pushing her plate away.

All of her ladies jump to their feet and prepare to dress her in the attire she chose the previous evening.

Everyone is glad to be doing something.

7:50 AM 19ᵗʰ Mary 1536

The Constable's Lodgings - The Tower of London

70 minutes until Anne Boleyn's execution

Thomas Cromwell has been in the Tower for the last fifteen minutes. He has already inspected the scaffold and is congratulating Kingston on the arrangements and his general diligence.

"The king will not be in attendance, I assume," enquires Kingston, praying that there will be no additional pressure on himself or the executioner.

Cromwell gives him a look that suggests Kingston already knows the answer. "No. He only wishes to know when it is done."

"His Majesty will hear the cannon," confirms Kingston, his eyes glancing towards the wharf.

Cromwell nods.

"And she will be allowed to speak?" asks Kingston.

"I believe that we will have to give her that right. But will she say the right things?" asks Cromwell, sipping a small mug of ale. "There can be no embarrassments. The lady has been known to be opinionated."

"It is my belief that she will say no ill about the king. I have heard none from her since she has been here. But I cannot believe that she will confess her guilt. If she will not do it before God in confession, then she will not do it for the crowd."

"It matters not. The people believe in her guilt." Cromwell says confidently, completely ignoring the information that has been coming back to him from the streets of London. "You will stop her if she speaks out of turn."

Kingston isn't quite as convinced as Cromwell of the mood of the people. His own reports tell him there is an element which believes the woman is wrongly tried.

"The lady's head will not be placed upon the bridge," Cromwell continues. "Bury her with due dignity as soon as you are able."

A flood of panic engulfs Kingston. He suddenly remembers something that has been lacking in his plans. Yet in the game of politics that he has been playing for as long as he can remember, he does not let it show.

Cromwell stands and Kingston follows suit, "Send your expenses for this matter as soon as you may. The king will want this matter settled in full before his wedding."

Cromwell leaves, giving his compliments to Kingston once again.

Kingston sends down for Captain Gwynn. The Captain appears within moments.

"You are to take two good men and make haste to the armoury. Remove the arrows from one strong chest.

Then carry the empty chest to the rear of the scaffold. Ensure it remains out of view and ensure you complete the task with the utmost haste."

Gwynn confirms he understands. But before he leaves he cannot help to ask, "What it is for, Sir?"

Kingston sees little point in lying, but does decide to lay the blame elsewhere. "The king has not made provision for a coffin."

Gwynn scampers off to complete the task.

Kingston smooths down his clothing and takes a moment to compose himself. He leaves to begin the hardest task he knows he will ever have to endure.

7:52 AM 19th May 1536

The Gates of the Tower of London

68 minutes until Anne Boleyn's execution

Bieito Caetano, a Portuguese merchant, is outside the gates of the Tower. He has already watched many well-to-do gentlemen and nobles enter the Tower that morning. Also the members of the various guilds in their blue robes. Now the normal, common people of the city are starting to shuffle their way in.

Just as Cromwell and Kingston had planned, word had clearly spread and a good number of people are coming to witness this unusual event. Bieito is aware that there was a ban on foreigners entering the Tower that day, but he could also see that the guards on the gate are overwhelmed with the numbers. He pulls down his hat and lowers his eyes to the ground for the guards to not easily see his olive skinned face, joining the rear of a group of English men.

There is no challenge from the guards.

Bieito is about to witness history and he is determined to record as many details as possible.

8.02AM 19th May 1536

The Queen's Lodgings - The Tower of London

Just less than one hour until Anne Boleyn's execution

Kingston enters the Queen's apartments.

Anne Boleyn stands before him. She is dressed in a brilliant red kirtle with a night robe of black damask, which is lined with fur. She has a netted coif over her hair to keep it in place. She looks remarkably beautiful and calm.

She has steadied herself and she is determined that her final moments will be ones of grace, dignity and humility. Yet there is something else. It is defiance. She will leave this world like a true queen and there will be no admission of guilt. Because guilty, of these crimes at least, she is not.

As Kingston looks on the face of the Lady in his charge the enormity of the situation hits him for the first time. For the first time in English history a queen of England will be executed. It was going to happen on his watch. It would happen here where the tower is white and another place is green. A thousand thoughts flood his mind at once. He will be the man remembered for leading the queen out to her fate. He knows that many on this earth would be joyful at this moment. The lady has offended many in the court and the land as a whole. But it isn't those on this earth that concerned him. It is what his God feels that worried him.

But he is steadfast in the resolve that he is doing his king's will. The king, who is God's messenger on Earth. He had sworn an oath to that very fact. The king's will must be obeyed, and with that he tries to speak, but stumbles a little with the words.

"My lady the hour approaches, I beseech you to make ready."

"Acquit yourself of your charge," Anne responds softly. "For I have been long prepared."

"You have a little while before we must depart, do now what you must with your ladies and your priest."

"Mister Skip will be allowed to accompany me?"

Technically speaking, as Anne had not confessed her guilt, a priest should be denied to her on the scaffold. He and Cromwell had not discussed the matter, but since there had been great preparation to ensure that the king would be seen to be handling matters above reproach, he sees little merit in denying her a priest.

"Indeed he will, Madam," confirmed Kingston. "As I say, there is time, but I must remain with you until the hour."

"It will be a comfort that you do, Sir. You have offered me much kindness these last days."

Kingston feels uncomfortable at the compliment. He has attempted to treat her with compassion. But to be thanked by the condemned woman seems wrong. He ignores the words and hands Anne a velvet purse, "A purse of twenty pounds for alms for the poor."

"The swordsman?" Anne bravely asks, after passing the purse to Lady Boleyn.

"The matter is already settled." Kingston confirms, then moved to stand by the door.

8:07 AM 19ᵗʰ May 1536

The Scaffold - The Tower of London

53 minutes until Anne Boleyn's execution

The swordsman of Calais is watching Captain's Gwynn's men carry an elm chest to the rear of the scaffold.

"For the lady," Gwynn confirms to the swordsman's enquiring glances.

The swordsman raises his eyebrows in disbelief. A queen? And she could not be given a real coffin? Maybe his own fee had left little over for anything as grand as a coffin.

He runs his finger around his collar. These new clothes were a little coarse. But Kingston had insisted that a new set be purchased for the occasion; he would foot the bill in addition to the swordsman's fee. Apparently everyone must look presentable and no-one, especially the swordsman, must stand out. The Constable had arranged for a tailor to take his and the boy's measurements not two hours after he arrived. The new garments were delivered in a short time. Today there would be no leather hood over the face and no tight-fitting doublet. The swordsman of Calais was to look like a well-to-do London gentleman.

The swordsman shifts his attention to his work area. The crowd is already growing. He estimates the number at some five hundred, but they are still flooding into the green. There will be many more present by the time the lady reaches the stairs. The crowd is naturally splitting itself into sections. There are the normal, everyday folk with their excited chatter. There are men dressed in blue and gold – he guesses these are representatives of the guilds and the merchants, many of whom are looking glum. Then a little way to the side are the officials and members of the royal court in their finery. As he looks out he felt no nerves and no inner conflict. He is a skilled professional being paid to do a job, just like those guild members out there. He had been doing this too long to feel regret. He wants it to be done, and then he will be home across the sea.

The scaffold is well made and draped in a good quality black cloth. Much of the front has been strewn with a liberal amount of straw to soak up the blood. The swordsman gestures to his boy kneeling down to unwrap the sword he had been carrying in a lightly oiled cloth.

"Don't wave it around in front of the crowd," the swordsman instructs in French.

The boy proceeds to ensure that straw is tightly packed around it so that the lady would not be able to see it when she arrived.

The swordsman grunts his approval and moves back to the rear where many of the other officials are starting to gather.

Walsingham is directing matters around the scaffold. He steps forward and places a thin white cushion on the straw. It would not do for the lady to hurt her knees kneeling on the wooden planks.

All is ready.

8:22AM 19ᵗʰ May 1536

The Queen's Lodgings - The Tower of London

A little over 40 minutes until the time of Anne Boleyn's execution

"Madam, it is time," declares Kingston softly after Skip finishes the latest prayer.

"Sir, would you do me one last honour?" Anne requests without rising from her knees.

"If I am able," agrees Kingston, keeping his vow to keep his prisoners calm.

"Will you join us in reciting the words that our Saviour taught us?"

Who would not seek comfort in the Lord at a moment like this? Kingston nods his consent and kneels alongside her.

The whole room recites the Lord's Prayer together.

8:24 AM 19ᵗʰ May 1536

The Scaffold, The Tower of London

36 minutes until Anne Boleyn's execution

Gregory Cromwell is watching his father with awe.

He is amazed at the ease with which his father speaks to great men like Norfolk and Suffolk. He has watched how man after man has come forward and offered Cromwell their hands, or been grateful for a word, or pressed a document to his hand. It suddenly dawns on him how important his father has become.

He is the centre of attention.

The puppet master.

With the queen dead, Gregory knows his father will now be in a position to pull all the strings.

8:26AM 19th May 1536

The Queen's Lodgings - The Tower of London

34 minutes until the time of Anne Boleyn's execution

Everyone rises to their feet after the recital of the Lord's Prayer.

Anne approaches Margaret Wyatt and hands her the little black leather prayer book she has kept with her over the last day, "A parting gift to remember me. I thank you with all my heart for your service." The two embrace for a moment.

Katherine Carey is on the verge of tears. Anne bends down taking the child's hand in hers and whispers in her ear, "Remember the blood that you have running through your veins, child. Be strong at this hour." Then after a moment of reflection she adds something more. "Tell your mother that I hope she will come to think kindly of me and remember the good times we shared. Tell her I am sorry for the offence that I gave her. Can you do that for me?"

Katherine nods her agreement and squeezes her aunt's hand. She manages to fight back the tears.

"Good girl," Anne says, before walking over to Mary Orchard, who cannot help but let a silent tear run down her face.

Anne turns and allows Mary to drape a cape of ermine, the symbol of royalty, over her shoulders. Henry may have legally removed her title, but with her cape she is going to make one last defiant statement that she is a queen. Finally, Anne has a black gable hood placed over her head. "Thank you Mary, for everything."

Mary cannot respond. The emotion of seeing the woman she has cared for since childhood walking out to her death is too much.

Anne addresses her aunt, Lady Boleyn. Both women know there is no affection between them and that the woman was placed with her to be a spy. But Anne now decides that she will entrust her with an important task in the hope that she, more than any of her other ladies, may have the courage to see it done. "Commend me to his Majesty and tell him he hath been ever constant in his career of advancing me. From a private gentlewoman he made me a marchioness, from a marchioness, a queen; and now that he hath left no higher degree of honour, he gives my innocency, the crown of martyrdom as a saint in Heaven."

Lady Boleyn nods, knowing that Kingston was already present to hear the words. She would allow him to report them to Cromwell if he wished. If Cromwell chose to deliver the message to the king so be it. She most certainly would not. But there was no need to tell that to the woman who was about to die.

Anne raises herself to her full height and looks back to her ladies. "Remember. Dignity. Shed no tears for me. For soon I will be in paradise."

She turns back to Kingston. "Let us proceed."

Kingston gives a bow and opens the door.

8:30 AM 19ᵗʰ 1536

Greenwich Palace, London

30 minutes until Anne Boleyn's execution

The Princess Elizabeth is finishing her breakfast, sitting under the great canopy of state that signifies she is the king's heir.

She is oblivious to the happenings unfolding in the Tower.

Lady Bryan is watching her carefully; she is amazed at how a girl so young manages to carry herself so well. It seems a shame that very soon her role in the kingdom will diminish significantly. She might have made a wonderful queen. Yet now this could not be.

Despite the reports she had received of the annulments of the marriage between the king and the queen, she had received no communication on a change of status of her charge. Until she did so, Elizabeth would continue to dine under the great canopy and she would be referred to as Princess.

However, Lady Bryan knows that it wouldn't be for much longer.

8:34 AM 19ᵗʰ May 1536

The Tower of London

A little over 25 minutes until Anne Boleyn's execution

The procession of Kingston, Anne, her ladies, and John Skip walk slowly down the steps of the Queen's lodgings into the courtyard situated between the Jewel house and the King's Hall.

Awaiting them are two hundred members of the guard together with Walsingham, who has left the scaffold after seeing all was in order, and the various other officers of the tower.

They waste no time. On Walsingham's orders the guard moves forward.

8:35 AM 19th May 1536

The Residence of the Imperial Ambassador

25 minutes until the execution of Anne Boleyn

Chapuys has at least four different Englishmen within the Tower ready to rush back and report on events. In addition, he expects a final report from Lady Kingston later that day.

He is a bundle of nervous energy.

The pain in his toe had kept him from sleep last night and at various moments he reflected on the injustice of the concubine's conviction. Then he would feel guilt that he had commiserated with her situation. After all, she had never commiserated with Queen Katherine or the Lady Mary.

Now, with the early spring sun in the sky, he feels different. The pain is starting to relent in his toe. He has determined that consumption of water seems to be the best treatment and he has been drinking it by the mugful. The piss pot has had to be emptied twice this morning already. Gone are the feelings of pity for the concubine.

Today Queen Katherine would get the justice that she deserved.

If it just happened to be based on a pack of lies and fabrications… then so be it.

8:37 AM 19ᵗʰ May 1536

The Tower of London

Just over 20 minutes until Anne Boleyn's execution

There is an audible gasp from the large crowd as the procession comes into view.

The procession moves slowly, allowing Anne and her ladies sufficient time to distribute alms from the purse that Kingston supplied. Many of those presented with coins from Anne herself offer words of comfort or blessing.

Bieito Caetano notes how beautiful she looks as she walks past him.

As she walks, Anne frequently turns to look behind her. Those present wonder if she is seeking reassurance from her ladies, or if she is looking for someone. The king perhaps? Or maybe she is looking for a messenger to arrive with a last minute reprieve. Few believe there will be one.

8:40 AM 19ᵗʰ May 1536

The King's Privy Apartments, Whitehall Palace, London

20 minutes until Anne Boleyn's execution

The doors are held open as Henry marches back into his apartments after attending Mass.

He is alone. His companions are all in attendance at the Tower.

He paces for a moment, unsure of how to handle one of his rare moments of solitude. His mind flicks to the Tower and he can see the frightened face of his former wife as she climbs the scaffold.

He freezes in horror as he suddenly realises the possibility that he might be a monster.

Then the warmth returns that he is simply carrying out justice. He had been wronged and justice must be served.

He sits down and turns his attention to the book that was open on his study table. Homer. He had never particularly liked Homer, but this morning it would have to do.

8:46AM 19ᵗʰ May1536

The Scaffold, The Tower of London

14 minutes until Anne Boleyn's execution

Kingston assists Anne up the five stairs to the platform of the scaffold. Her ladies and John Skip follow carefully behind.

The officers of the Tower have already ascended the scaffold, and the swordsman in his new clothing is indistinguishable from the others. Only the swordsman's assistant, on account of his age, might be identified, if Anne was so inclined. However, identifying the man that would send her to heaven is not yet on her mind.

Instead, she turns to Kingston, "Sir, I beg leave to speak to the people. I do promise that I will not offer a word that is not good to His Majesty."

"Indeed, Madam," Kingston confirms with a small wave.

"Please, do not give the signal for my death until I have spoken that which I hath a mind to say."

Once again Kingston confirms that this is acceptable, and takes a step back, leaving Anne alone in the middle of the platform.

She takes a moment to gather her thoughts, and the murmur of expectation calms into an uneasy silence as the crowd waits to hear her words.

"Good Christian people, I have not come here to preach a sermon; I have come here to die, for according to the law and by the law I am judged to die, and therefore I will speak nothing against it," She begins, in a slightly uneasy voice. She pauses for a second before finding courage which is immediately evident in the strength and confidence of her words. "I am come hither to accuse no man, nor to speak of that whereof I am accused and condemned to die, but I pray God save the King and send him long to reign over you, for a gentler nor a more merciful prince was there never, and to me he was ever a good, a gentle and sovereign lord. And if any person will meddle of my cause, I require them to judge the best. And thus I take my leave of the world and of you all, and I heartily desire you all to pray for me."

Watching with the various members of the court, Cromwell can't help but think it a fine speech. One that he would have been proud of writing himself. Despite his burly physique and his uncompromising, ruthless character, he began to feel something strange — the pangs of regret. Once he was Anne's champion, "her man" as she had called it. But in the later months it had simply become a choice of him or her. If he hadn't engineered her downfall, she would have engineered his. He had no option, and he was a master at his craft.

The words are moving, so much so that many in the crowd begin to cry. Antony is one such person who was so moved that he records the words once he reaches his home. He had not even planned on attending that morning, but was caught up in the crowds and followed along to see what the excitement was.

Anne turns to her maids and slowly, step by step, they undress her so the swordsman could do his task. Mary comes forward and carefully removes the ermine cape, ensuring at all times to maintain her lady's dignity. Anne herself removes her gable and hands it to Lady Boleyn. Then Katherine Carey comes forward and hands Anne a white linen cap. The net coif that she is already wearing means her hair is easily gathered within.

The Queen of England is almost ready.

8:50AM 19ᵗʰ May 1536

Peterborough Abbey

10 minutes until the time of Anne Boleyn's execution

John Chambers, Abbot of Peterborough Abbey, is walking hurriedly through the cloisters.

He was summoned just moments ago by a red faced novice who claims there has been a miracle.

As he approaches the quire he sees monks on their knees in a union of collective prayer. They are all gathered around the tomb of Queen Katherine, the king's first wife.

The tapers which surround the tomb are unusually all lit.

"The tapers. They lit up of their own accord. No man put flame to them. It is the will of God," the novice whispers in the abbot's ear.

The abbot looks dumbstruck for a moment. A miracle indeed. What could have caused it? With no answer to his questions, he can do only one thing. He falls to knees and joins the others in giving thanks to God.

8:55AM 19th May 1536

The Scaffold, The Tower of London

5 minutes until Anne Boleyn's execution

Anne is speaking to her ladies for the final time. Lady Boleyn has shrunk into the background. There would be no final farewell between them.

"Ladies, while I lived you showed yourselves to be ever diligent in my service. Now you are present at my last hour and my mortal agony,
Be as faithful to me as you always have been. With my miserable death, please do not forsake me. I beg your pardon for any harshness or swift temper I have shown to you, I meant it not. Remember that I have always been faithful to the King's Grace and please remember not this hour, but happier times when I was your queen and mistress. Please, in your prayers to the Lord Jesu, forget not to pray for my soul."

The ladies nod and the three of them can hold back the tears no more. Lady Boleyn looks on with scorn for she believes that the woman deserves the death she will receive.

Anne turns away from her grieving women for fear that she herself will break down in tears.
Kingston nods to the line-up of officials, and the swordsman steps forward and kneels before Anne. "Madam, I crave your Majesty's pardon for I am ordered to do this duty."

"I give it willing," Anne responds in French.

"Then, Madam, I beg you to kneel and say your prayers."

Very slowly Anne takes a step forward and very carefully she kneels on the thin, white cushion. She takes great care to fasten her clothing around her feet: the last thing she desires is at the final moment dignity escaping her.

Margaret then comes forward, her eyes still pouring tears, and completes one final task. She blindfolds Anne with a linen cloth and gives her a reassuring pat on the shoulders before stepping back to join the other weeping women.

Anne is now blinded and moves her head around to attempt to work out the movements of the swordsman.

"Do not fear," he says, "I will wait until you tell me."

But right now, at that moment, despite the defiance, despite the show of dignity, despite the moving words, now at the very last, fear is what Anne felt.

Her hand rises to her hair to tuck in stray strands that had somehow escaped the coif and cap, as if a lock of hair might impede the strike of the swordsman.

The need for prayer hit her, "Jesu, have pity on my soul. My God, have pity on my soul." Then she repeats the words, "O Jesu, receive my spirit. Christ, receive my spirit."

The Lord Mayor of London, Sir John Aleyn, falls to his knees in his own prayer, moved by such a sight.

Those around him follow suit. And in a matter of moments the thousand or so that had gathered are on their knees. Even in the section that contains the nobles and officials of court, one by one men fall to their knees. Cromwell looks around him and sees no reason not to do likewise. In the end only the Duke of Suffolk, Charles Brandon, and The Duke of Richmond and Somerset, Henry Fitzroy, remain standing in mutual loathing of the woman about to die.

Such a sight is unprecedented. Kingston looks out from the scaffold in wonder. The swordsman, the very picture of calm, pauses to look out on the crowd.

And all the time, Anne Boleyn waits for the fatal blow to strike.

"O Lord God, have pity on my soul! To Christ I commend my soul."

8:59AM 19ᵗʰ 1536

The Bell Tower, The Tower of London

1 minute until the time of Anne Boleyn's execution.

Thomas Wyatt cannot see the scaffold site and he is glad.

He had heard the crowd as it grew in number, and then the gasp that occurred when the lady came into view. He then heard the hush and the lone female voice speaking, although he was too far away to hear the words.

He knows the blow would come soon.

The woman he has loved would be dead.

The tears begin to flow and Wyatt never wants them to stop.

9:03 AM 19ᵗʰ May 1536

The Scaffold, The Tower of London

Despite the fact there are over one thousand people packed in front of Caesar's Tower there is silence. Everyone in the crowd except Suffolk and Richmond are on their knees.

The blindfolded Anne Boleyn is kneeling on a thin cushion, repeating prayers under her breath. At the back, three of her ladies cannot control their tears.

Silently the swordsman takes a step to the side and shouts out across the scaffold to his assistant, "Boy, fetch me my sword."

Over on the stairs of the scaffold, the swordsman's assistant deliberately makes a noise.

Anne's head immediately turns towards the noise, blindly searching for the source.

At the same time the swordsman bends and pulls out the sword that was hidden earlier. It was a short blade of just over three feet in length, with a rounded tip. The double-edge blade glinted in the early morning sunlight as he pulled it back.

Anne Boleyn is still searching for the source of the boy's noise and does not notice a thing.

Without hesitation the swordsman swings the blade forward in a glorious curving arc.

Anne's smitten head falls into the straw.

9:04AM 19th May 1536

Tower Wharf

Moments after Anne Boleyn's execution

Captain Bray has been standing on the wharf since dawn. He knew that today of all days the folk of London, great and low alike, would be awaiting him to do his job.

His arm has been raised for the past five minutes in anticipation. His eyes do not move from watching his mark.

Finally, the signal comes and Bray turns to his men and drops his arm.

As one, the wharf cannons fire.

The city of London knows the deed is done.

The apartments of the Earl of Wiltshire, Whitehall Palace

As he hears the cannon, Thomas Boleyn finally closes his eyes.

The game of power that he has been playing for years is over.

He has lost the most valuable thing he has ever possessed — his children. Two are dead, lifeless corpses without heads. The third is estranged, disowned, and forgotten. He thinks it strange that the child that chose to walk away from the game turned out to be the happiest.

He wonders if maybe he had it wrong all of these years. Maybe he should have just settled for what life had in store for him. After all, life had dealt him a favourable hand in the first instance. But it wasn't enough, he had wanted more. When a crown was dangled before him, he found it impossible not to reach out and try to touch. Or at least, order his daughters so.

The blame was not his. He had assured himself of that over these dark days.

It was Anne's fault. All of it.

Why couldn't she just give the king what he wanted? A son. It was a simple enough requirement.

Why couldn't she keep her mouth shut and her opinions to herself?

Why couldn't she close her eyes and endure?

In the end maybe Anne was too much her father's daughter and being a queen consort simply wasn't enough for her. Maybe she wanted to rule herself?

But it wasn't his fault. Thomas Boleyn knows that. Anne was to blame. It was she that had brought destruction and shame on them all.

But even then, at that moment, when all has been lost, Thomas Boleyn ponders if there might just be a way back.

The Archbishop's Private Chapel, Lambeth Palace

Deep within the walls of Lambeth Palace, the deep thud of the cannon could still be heard.

Thomas Cranmer is at prayer, as he has been since dawn. He was not to be disturbed, unless there was favourable news from the Tower. He expected none and therefore he was not disturbed.

As the cannon sounds, Cranmer knows the reformers had lost their greatest champion.

It was she, sweet Anne, that had the ear of the king. It was she that whispered thoughts, ideas, and dreams into his royal head in the dead of night. She planted the seeds and the king would nurture them.

Without her what would become of their reforms?

Already word was that Henry was considering an Imperial Alliance. Would that thrust Henry back into the arms of Rome and a time of darkness? Cromwell offered little comfort despite his reforming leanings. Cromwell could have stopped all of this if he desired. But he didn't desire. He wanted to be closer to the king than ever. He wanted to overthrow the woman that had helped raise them all up. Cromwell wanted the king's ear to himself.

His sweet lady was dead. The woman who had raised him up by pushing his cause and encouraging the king to appoint him as Archbishop of Canterbury, despite the fact that he had never held high ecclesiastical office.

In turn, he could do nothing to save her.

Strangely, he doesn't feel sorrow. He doesn't feel anger. He feels shame.

Greenwich Palace

The Princess Elizabeth hears the cannon just like everyone else. In fact, it makes the little girl jump as she has been playing obliviously.

Lady Bryan, who is with her, gives a warning glance at the other women who are present. After a moment's pause and the realisation that it has finally happened, all those present simply continue with their tasks like nothing has occurred.

The child does the same and clutches her doll as though her life hasn't changed a bit. Unfortunately for her, it has. Thankfully, Elizabeth knows nothing about it.

Alexander Johnson's Inn, Cheapside

Alexander Johnson and his wife, Mary, are cleaning up from the night before. Mary had wished to go to the Tower to see the woman's death. Alexander had refused it, knowing that the inn must be ready.

Even last night the place was packed with people flocking to celebrate the downfall of the woman that pretended to be queen.

Now, as the cannon fires, Alexander knows the place will be packed twice as deeply by noon. The couple smiles to themselves. The queen was hated and now she was dead. The people of London will wish to celebrate. They can almost feel the weight of coin even now.

The residence of the Imperial Ambassador

Eustace Chapuys smiles wryly as the sound of the cannon reaches him.

The king of England has finally seen sense. The whore is dead. He hopes that Queen Katherine finally has peace.

Despite the triumph, Chapuys knows there is still work to be done. He must push for an English alliance with his master. The French loving whore would no longer be an obstacle. He knows there is finally a chance to have Mary reinstated to the line of succession. He knows that she has some friends at court, and no doubt that number would increase in the next few weeks, but he knows that he must be her guide.

Shortly the Englishmen whom he had paid will arrive to give their reports. Lady Kingston will undoubtedly provide her own view of the concubine's last morning. Chapuys hopes to read of tears, confessions, and pain. After all, it is no more than the she-devil deserved.

He decides that it is time to break his fast. He will need his strength in the hours to come. There is much to be done.

The Seymour Residence, Chelsea

Jane Seymour hears the cannon and shudders. She knows that her former mistress's head is lying in sawdust. She isn't sorry.

Anne had been harsh and cutting to all of the ladies in her service. Once news of the king's advances became known to her, Jane had received even more of Anne's venom. It was not as though she were able to resist the advances of the king. She was not the first of Anne's ladies that he had chased and caught. Anne knew the game; she had been playing it long enough.

When it became clear that the king was displeased with Anne, many at court considered her a suitable replacement. Her father and brothers had immediately embraced these overtures. After they decided they wanted Jane as queen, they coached her on how to win a king. It wasn't a hardship to Jane. Henry was the picture of manhood, and a crown as the final reward only made it more appealing.

Yet now, at that moment, after all her work, the prospect of becoming Henry's queen isn't appealing at all.

No, she isn't sorry that Anne is dead. She is sorry that it is the result of Henry's determination to be rid of her. He had cast aside two wives already. What is to say that he won't cast aside a third?

Jane already knows the answer. Only one thing will assure her long-term future and security.

She must give birth to a boy.

The king's privy apartments, Whitehall

It is over.

Henry didn't expect to feel like this. He had been tense all morning and had insisted that he be alone. Now it is over and he feels relief.

He does not reflect on the sentiment. He had loved her once. But no longer.

She had manipulated him for long enough with her games. She had bewitched him. And then she had publicly shamed him, making him a cuckold in his own royal palace. He had raised her and now he has brought her down.

Now the cannon has fired. Now it is done and he can marry again, seeing to the important business of ensuring the succession.

Soon his gentlemen will return. He wonders about a game of tennis — or maybe a hunt?

He glances down at the Bible he has been attempting to read that morning. The pages are open, but he cannot remember a thing he has read. He saw the Bible was open to the book of Leviticus. He slams it shut. Leviticus. Look at the good that had brought him.

It is over. He need think of her no more.

9:05 AM 19ᵗʰ May 1536

The Scaffold, The Tower of London

Moments after Anne Boleyn's execution.

The echo of the cannon still resonates around Tower Green.

Sir John Spelman is at the front of the crowd. He has witnessed executions in the past. In fact, he was present at Tower Hill to see the deaths of the five men that defiled the queen — but nothing has made him as repulsed as what he was just seen.

He can't move his eyes from the severed head of Anne Boleyn, lying in the straw. As he stares at the head he is sure that the lips are still moving in prayer. After a few long seconds they grow still and one of the queen's ladies covers the head with a white cloth.

Spelman will see the head and the moving lips many times in his nightmares after that moment.

9:06 AM 19ᵗʰ May 1536

Peterborough Abbey

Minutes after Anne Boleyn's execution

The monks are still at prayer around the tomb of Queen Katherine.

Then, with no man approaching them and as if a sudden gust of wind did sweep through, the tapers extinguish.

There is an audible gasp from those assembled.

The monks simply pray harder.

9:07AM 19ᵗʰ May 1536

Hunsdon House

Minutes after Anne Boleyn's execution

A strange feeling of calm rushes over the Lady Mary.

Despite the fact that she will not receive confirmation until later that evening, she knows that it is done.

Her enemy is dead. Her mother can finally rest in peace.

What now for her? A reconciliation with her father? Her restoration to the succession?

At present her father has no male heir.

Maybe one day she might be Queen. It seems almost unbelievable. Yet somehow she knows it will come to be.

9:10 AM 19th May 1536

The Scaffold, The Tower of London

6 minutes after the execution of Anne Boleyn

Kingston is amazed by how quickly the crowd seems to dissipate after the main event. He guesses that they had all rushed off to get on with their lives or to report what they had seen to their friends and family. Some will be making visits to important personages to report to them on the events of the morning.

One man in particular will be visiting an important personage to give him a report. That man is Cromwell and Kingston is glad that he doesn't have to do the job himself. No doubt Norfolk, Suffolk, and Richmond would all give their reports to the king as well. But Kingston was glad that there was nothing ill to report.

Cromwell ascends the stairs, completely ignoring requests from various members of the court for a word. They know that Cromwell now has no rival in the land. The nobles may despise the base born brute, but they know that he is the king's man. The power and the influence are his. Cromwell congratulates Kingston on his handling of the matter and assures him the king will be most pleased.

Kingston feels no satisfaction in the compliment. He simply feels relief that it is done. And tiredness. Overwhelming tiredness.

Cromwell does not glance in the direction of the body. He reminds Kingston to submit the expenses without delay and then leaves to report to the king.

Kingston still has a number of duties to attend to before he can finally say that this is finished.

Lady Boleyn is attempting to organise the three other ladies. She wants this to be finished as much as Kingston. The three are inconsolable and are fully aware of where Lady Boleyn's allegiance has been. They are not inclined to obey.

Kingston approaches Lady Boleyn and offers a small bow as greeting, "I will send Captain Gwynn and his men to assist you."

"No, Sir," interrupts Margaret. "They cannot assist yet. I won't let any man touch her."

Kingston nods his head, "They will not touch her, madam. I assure you."

Kingston speaks to the Captain, who instructs the men to bring forth the chest. Kingston decides it would be best to supervise the final act in this remarkable play.

The crowd has all but left, just a handful of morbid onlookers watch. Kingston is glad: the arrow chest isn't his finest moment. Margaret stares in disbelief at the chest, as if to say, *Are we really putting the Queen of England in there?*

Very carefully, the ladies pick up the body and lay it within the chest. Fortunately, it just fits. Mary Orchard retrieves the head and lays it with the body. They step back and allow Captain Gwynn's men to carry it to the church.

Kingston stops Lady Boleyn. "The garments she was wearing are required by the king."

"Seriously?" demands Lady Boleyn. "Has he not had enough?"

"Seriously." Kingston confirms with a glare before marching down the stairs.

9:45 AM 19ᵗʰ May 1536

St Peter ad Vincula, The Tower of London

Almost 45 minutes after Anne Boleyn's execution

The body of Anne Boleyn has been undressed and is shrouded in a white cloth. It remains in the arrow chest.

Lady Boleyn looks distastefully at the pile of bloodied clothing that have been removed and wonders what on earth the king plans to do with it.

Katherine Carey is seated a little way away from the makeshift coffin. It has all been too much for the young girl, and Lady Boleyn, in a rare act of compassion, decides that she need play no further part in the proceedings.

Margaret and Mary have regained their composure; they know that these are the final tasks they will do for their mistress and are determined to see her buried with the dignity due to the queen.

Lady Boleyn starts walking around the church. After a few moments it is obvious that there have been no arrangements for a place for her to be buried. Neither does there seem to be a priest available to say Mass. She can hardly believe it. Even after death the woman is still causing her problems.

She goes to the door where Captain Gwynn and his men are still standing guard. She tells the Captain to fetch Kingston immediately.

Keen not to upset the formidable lady, Gwynn rushes off to do as she demands.

St Peter ad Vincula, The Tower of London

Almost one and a half hours after Anne Boleyn's execution

Kingston looks a broken man when he eventually answers Lady Boleyn's summons.

Since the execution he had found himself entertaining Suffolk, Norfolk, and Richmond, all of whom were keen to tell him how thankful the king was for his diligence. This was all very well, but it didn't provide him with the one thing he really needed at that moment, which was sleep! No sooner had the noble guests left then the hangman of Calais also bid him farewell. He had changed from the new clothing Kingston had insisted be purchased back to the clothes he had on when he arrived. Kingston noted that the new clothing was firmly packed away to go home with him. Kingston thanked him for his service and professionalism. In return he said that Kingston always knew where he was if his services were required again.

Kingston prayed that this would not be the case. He doubted he could go through this performance a second time.

Now Lady Boleyn is greeting him at the door to the church with a face like thunder.
"There is no grave and no priest," she hissed.

Kingston's heart sinks. Like the coffin, this is another matter that he had neglected. No doubt word would get back to Cromwell.

A grave could be dug, but the issue of the priest was complex. The queen had not confessed to her crimes. Technically she not should have been allowed a priest on the scaffold, but Cromwell had relaxed the convention. Kingston isn't sure if he can find a priest quickly to do the task.

"I can get one of her chaplains to perform the service," offers Lady Boleyn, holding out an olive branch. She too is fully aware of the conventions and knows what Kingston is throwing about in his mind. She wants this matter resolved as quickly as possible, and working with Kingston seems to be the best solution.

Kingston nods his agreement, "I will arrange for some men to dig the grave."

11:02 AM 19ᵗʰ May 1536

St Peter ad Vincula, The Tower of London

Two hours after Anne Boleyn's execution

Two men, Samuel and Thomas, have arrived to commence work on the grave. Captain Gwynn is supervising, not wishing the two men to be left alone with the ladies and the body of the queen.

These are the same men that dug the grave for Lord Rochford a few days ago. They know just how to lift the flagstones with iron crowbars to gain access to the earth beneath.

In hushed tones the three men decide that, in view of the crimes for which they had been convicted, it would not be correct to lay the queen to rest next to her brother. So flagstones are removed at the opposite end of the altar to where the body of George Boleyn already lay.

12:35 PM 19ᵗʰ May 1536

St Peter ad Vincula, The Tower of London

Around three and half hours after Anne Boleyn's execution

Father Thirlwall gives a simple blessing over the arrow chest that contains the body of the Queen of England. It is after noon and therefore Mass cannot be celebrated.

With as much dignity as they can muster, Captain Gwynn and his men lower the chest into the shallow grave that had only been completed minutes before. The workers stand to the side, hardly believing that they are present at the burial of a queen.

Katherine, Margaret, and Mary are once more in tears. Lady Boleyn remains as stony faced as ever, although she does continue to watch young Katherine. She hopes that these events won't scar her too much. Lady Kingston stands with Lady Boleyn: they had shared the duties of a spy since Anne's imprisonment and it seemed fitting that they complete this last shift together.

Finally, at the back of the church in the shadows stands Sir William Kingston. He had felt compelled to attend and ensure all was finally done.

He knows in his heart that even though the king's will has been done, justice has not been served. The bravery with which the lady had met her end was something to behold.

He watched as the chest disappears from view and then turns to leave the church.

As the door shuts behind him, he suddenly feels relief.

1:00 PM 19ᵗʰ May 1536

The Bell Tower, The Tower of London

Just less than four hours after Anne Boleyn's execution

Thomas Wyatt's tears have dried and now he is composing his thoughts about the downfall of the woman he had once loved.

The words flow…

So freely wooed, so dearly bought,
So soon a queen, so soon low brought,
Hath not been seen, could not be thought.
O! What is Fortune?

As slippery as ice, as fading as snow,
Like unto dice that a man doth throw,
Until it arises he shall not know
What shall be his fortune!

They did her conduct to a tower of stone,
Wherein she would wail and lament her alone,
And condemned be, for help there was none.
Lo! Such was her fortune.

He lays down his pen and reads again.

Then the images flood his mind and he fears the fate that may await him.

Author's Notes

The subject of the downfall of Anne Boleyn has been a hugely popular one over the years. While her rise to become Henry's wife and queen took many years, her downfall was so swift it could be measured in days. May 1536 remains one of the most remarkable and shocking months in English history.

This book has attempted to take the vast amount of documented evidence from those final days and arrange it into a timeline. As you will have seen, the period covered in the book does extend a little longer than twenty-four hours. This is because what was happening just outside that twenty-four-hour window was so compelling. Plus, *Anne Boleyn - The Final 35 Hours* isn't quite as catchy a title.

Clearly, the book also blends fact and fiction. The fiction elements attempt to convey what the principal players in this situation were doing and how they were feeling as the momentous events unfolded. Where possible I have tried to keep matters that are considered pure legend out of the book. However, on a couple of instances the "story" is simply too good to leave out. The story that the tapers lit of their own accord around the tomb of Katherine of Aragon is one such example. I have, however, changed the time period on this event in order that it fits in context with the unfolding story.

As I was arranging the evidence, there was something that did immediately strike me as odd. This was the fact that the execution was postponed on more than one occasion. There seems to have been no proper, formal plan for the execution that was due to be held on the 18th May. We know that Cromwell's instruction to clear the tower of strangers before the execution took place arrived just minutes before the scheduled time of the execution on the 18th May. However, from what we can determine, Kingston had not yet gone to escort the queen to the place of execution. There were also no notable figures from court present in the Tower that morning, nor did there seem to be the great crowds that attended the following day. Clearly Cromwell was not present at the Tower, as he was sending messages to Kingston to delay the execution.

It offers the question: why was the execution of the Queen of England seemingly so badly organised?

Half of me wonders if the execution was really due to take place on the eighteenth at all. Why was it when the messenger arrived from Cromwell, Kingston was not even with the queen? Yet twenty-four hours later he arrives almost a full hour ahead of time to ensure she arrives at the scaffold at the appointed time. Why were there no leading players from court at the Tower? Suffolk and Richmond would have surely desired to see the execution take place for the reasons already covered in the text: indeed, they, along with Norfolk, were present on the nineteenth. Why were they not present on the eighteenth? It does seem strange.

Kingston was clearly under extreme stress, as the matters he had been forced to deal with were unprecedented. This can be seen in the way he neglected to provide for a coffin for the body of the queen and did not made arrangements for the burial of the body. Simply, there was too much to do in too little time. Cromwell, the other man who had the burden of arranging matters, was probably exhausted. It is now a widely held belief that he was the engineer of Anne's downfall. It was a huge gamble. Had it failed then all would have been lost for him and it would likely have been him awaiting execution that morning. Basically, the two men who were required to oversee the task were stressed, overworked, and exhausted. There was no procedure to follow, and they were making matters up as they went along.

What I found really interesting is how, in the space of just twenty-four hours, Kingston and Cromwell went from what was essentially a shambles to conducting a huge "spectacle" with over one thousand people present. A "spectacle" that, according to the numerous independent reports of events, seemed to go without incident. The amount of work that went into those final twenty-four hours must have been phenomenal. What I also see is the great compassion that seems to have been shown by Kingston to his charge. His wife was clearly no fan of Anne and we can presume that Kingston himself shared her views, but his professionalism in his dealings with the queen were without question.

There are many different reports and journal entries regarding Anne Boleyn's final public appearance. Some were written by those in attendance, others by those hearing information second hand. All give slightly different versions of events. There are numerous recorded versions of Anne's final speech, for example. I have chosen a commonly repeated account for this book. However, one thing is clear from all the accounts written about that fateful final hour: Anne faced her final moments with great bravery and dignity. I have attempted to get that across in the book.

The accounts of Anne's execution all vary to a degree. For the purposes of an entertaining read, I chose to use the account of those watching falling to their knees. Whether this really occurred we will never know, but it adds to the drama of the story.

Trying to capture how the principal players felt at this time was one of my chief aims when starting this book.

I had been taught, incorrectly, at school, that Henry was out hunting when the execution took place. I wanted to try to get into his head and get a feel of what he really thought about the execution of the woman he had once moved heaven and earth for. It seems that the king really believed in Anne's guilt and had convinced himself that he was the injured party. Therefore, we can assume that he believed the fate that met his former wife was just. We know very little about how Henry spent his time during Anne's final twenty-four hours. We know that during the imprisonment and trial Henry did not go out in public, probably on the recommendation of Cromwell. However, his visit to the Seymours did occur, as did a similar one the following night, after the execution.

Some of the players' feelings were easy to determine. Lady Mary, for example, was obviously ecstatic, Cranmer clearly distraught. Others were harder to get a grip on. Chapuys comes over as a man torn. Anne was his mortal enemy and he rejoices at her downfall, yet we know from his dispatches that he doesn't believe for an instant that she is guilty and has grave concerns about the lack of evidence presented at her trial. He freely states that no person met their fate as bravely as she. So while delighted at her fall, he praised her in the same breath. Thomas Boleyn is another who is hard to judge. Was he really as cold and heartless as we are made to believe? Surely he would have felt something at the death of two of his children? It is almost impossible to tell. We know that other than the loss of one major office, he emerged from the scandal without harm.

Cromwell appears to be as efficient and calculating as we have been led to believe over recent years. We seem to accept that he was the mastermind behind Anne's downfall. During this period, he would have carried a great deal of administrative burden on his shoulders. It is unlikely that he had much time to "feel" anything at all. He may have had the odd pang of regret, but he was painfully aware that if he did not do away with the queen then she would do away with him.

The matter of Anne's ladies needs to be addressed. I have named the ladies serving on Anne based on fact and supposition. We know that on her imprisonment in the Tower four ladies were waiting on Anne. All of whom had been supplied by Cromwell and were to report back to him everything that Anne said or did. These ladies were all "old" or at least mature women, we even know their names:

Elizabeth Wood, Lady Boleyn - She was Anne's aunt, the wife of Thomas Boleyn's brother.

Lady Anne Shelton - Again Anne's aunt, this time the sister of Thomas Boleyn.

Mary Orchard - Anne's former nurse and someone that she would have been familiar with.

Margaret Coffin - The wife of her own Master of the horse.

In addition, Lady Kingston was required to spend time with the queen and report matters to her husband.

However, we also know from the reports of the actual execution that many of the accounts refer to Anne's young ladies accompanying her to the scaffold. None of the women that were waiting on her prior to the trial could possibly be described as young. Hence, it stands to reason that at some point after the trial some or all of the ladies were changed. It has always been "tradition" that Katherine Carey was one of her young ladies. Another young woman often quoted as being present was Margaret Wyatt. Of course there is no definitive proof that either of these women were Anne's ladies on that fateful day. However, it seems they are as good as any young women to include in this account. In short I decided to retain Lady Boleyn and Mary Orchard for these final 24 hours, together with Lady Kingston who was obviously still present in the Tower. I then added Katherine and Margaret. This decision may upset some people, but a choice had to be made.

How did Anne feel on those final days? How does a condemned person feel? Especially one that was almost certainly innocent of the charges which convicted her. I don't know and I hope never to do so. We can only imagine that there was a mixture of shock, fear, and anger. Yet she managed to keep her composure and died with the utmost dignity.

Quite simply her memory will live forever.

I hope you enjoyed the book.

You may email me on
marcellamayfairauthor@gmail.com

My website is

marcellamayfair.com

OUT NOW

Richard III - The Final 24 Hours

A Taster

6:03 AM 21st August 1485
The White Boar Inn, Leicester
*27 hours and twelve minutes until the death of
Richard III*

Richard III of England woke after a decent night's
sleep.

He has to admit to himself that he has awoken in far
more luxurious accommodations than the White Boar Inn
in this lifetime. On the other hand, he reflects that has
awoken in far worse as well. He had certainly awoken in
some hovels when on campaign with his elder brother
Edward IV, or during those dark and bleak months of
exile when the turncoat Warwick helped restore the
simple minded Henry VI to the throne. *The Kingmaker*
many people had called Warwick. At that point Richard
had simply called him a bastard. It was a little harsh,
considering that he had been brought up in the man's
household and had considered him a second father. He
had even married his daughter! But for turning against
the House of York he was a bastard. *The Kingmaker*
wouldn't be interfering in the current games that were
going on for the throne: he'd been dead for well over a
decade, killed at the battle of Barnet while trying to flee
like a coward.

The man that now held the kingmaker's title, Earl of Warwick, was his grandson and Richard's own nephew. He was a simple witted boy and also wouldn't be partaking in this round of games. As the son of Richard's attained brother, the Duke of Clarence, the new Earl of Warwick had no rights to the throne. Yet, Richard was fully aware that attainders could be reversed in Parliament. Despite his lack of wits, his nephew's title and heritage made him a risk. Some ambitious fool could attempt to rule through him. This was why young Warwick was up at Sheriff Hutton in Richard's heartland of Yorkshire. There he was firmly out of the way and under the watchful gaze of some of the king's most trusted men. As a king without a living son, Richard had to make sure that all potential claimants to his crown were kept close to the throne. Whilst he was dealing with this insignificant and troublesome Welshman, it was quite possible others were plotting new schemes in dark rooms elsewhere.

Richard had plans for the other principle claimant: his brother's daughter, Elizabeth. She too was safely out of harm's way at Sheriff Hutton castle. Richard was only too aware of the Welshman's public declaration the previous Christmas in Reims that he would marry Elizabeth of York and take the crown for himself. He was also fully aware of the plotting that had been going on between the two elderly witches of the royal court, his brother's widow, Elizabeth Woodville, and the vile, scheming, single minded Margret Beaufort. They were the powerhouses behind the Welshman's ambitions. If their two children married and took the throne, then they would see the final unification of the Houses of York and Lancaster. Woodville would like nothing better than to see Richard fall. Even Richard couldn't blame her.

Once the Welshman was defeated, which would only be in a matter of days, then Richard himself would marry his niece — after the formalities of a dispensation from the Pope had been granted of course. Only recently he had been forced to deny that he was planning on marrying Elizabeth of York. But now that his own queen, Anne, was dead, there was nothing in his path to stop him. There was also the possibility of a foreign princess, but portraits lie. Richard had seen Elizabeth; he knew of her beauty and he was smitten. Advantageously, she would be removed as a player for his throne.

The great game had been played in England for nigh on thirty years. Thousands upon thousands of men had lost their lives in the continual quest for power and glory. Now there were so few claimants to the throne left alive that the ludicrous House of Lancaster had been forced to serve up Margret Beaufort's Welsh son Henry Tudor as their saviour. Someone had to physically sit down with Richard and show him on a family tree how Henry Tudor had a claim to the throne. Richard had laughed when the connections to the crown were pointed out: an illegitimate female line to Edward III. No one in England would accept this man as their king, he had thought. Yet, on this point Richard was mistaken, as clearly some Englishmen did accept it: even now, Henry Tudor rode at the head of a large army not many miles from where he sat.

But Richard was confident. He had every right to be. Richard was a battle hardened military general. The Duke of Norfolk was by his side, as were the Earls of Northumberland, Kent, Shrewsbury, Lincoln, and West Murland.

The Welshman had never fought in a battle. He had spent his life hiding in exile. His only significant noble support came in the form of the Earl of Oxford and of course, his wizened uncle, Jasper. And yet Richard's spies had brought news of defections as Tudor had made his way from Pembroke, Rhys Ap Thomas and Thomas Mitton among them. Milton had vowed that Tudor would only enter England over his body — so much for that vow. Tudor's forces were growing, and Richard had to engage and put an end to this sooner rather than later.

Despite the growing forces of his rival, Richard knew he would win. The odds were still massively stacked in his favour. He was experienced in warfare. He had the nobles. He would march out of Leicester by nine in the morning and choose the ground on which they would fight. He was the one wearing the crown. He was king. He couldn't lose to an insignificant Welshman with a fool's claim on the English throne.

But in amongst his confidence Richard sensed something else.

Doubt.

That doubt focused on one thing:

What was Lord Thomas Stanley planning to do?

6:15 AM 21st August 1485
The Cistercian Abby at Merevale, near Atherstone
27 hours until the death of Richard III

Thomas, Lord Stanley reflected on the clandestine meeting that had ended a little more than half an hour ago.

There were fewer better places that helped with the matter of reflection than the calmness of a Cistercian Abbey. Thomas was far less accustomed than his current wife at spending hours in religious devotion. Ever since their marriage, Margret Beaufort had spent more hours at pray than any other person he had ever met. There was no love or passion in their marriage. There never had been, and never would be. It was mutually beneficial political union. As one of the last remaining Lancastrian figures Margret Beaufort had needed a place of safety within the establishment of the House of York. Thomas Stanley had always been a Yorkist king's man, for her he was the perfect choice. The properties, lands, and wealth that Margret Beaufort had brought with her as the Beaufort heiress and on the back of two previous marriages had made the continual plotting and scheming that also came with her just about bearable. It wasn't a match made in heaven, but rather one forged on the bloody and brutal political landscape of the royal houses of England.

Whilst Edward IV was on the throne there was no chance that Margret would have managed to twist Thomas' mind with her treasonous schemes of bringing her exiled son home and to the throne she believed was his. But the colossus that was King Edward was dead, a simple fever doing the job that countless battles could not. Richard, Duke of Gloucester had then usurped the throne from the fingers of his own nephews, in an instant betraying the loyalty to his brother that during his reign had been unquestioned. No one had seen the little Princes for almost three years. Margret had it on good authority that the boys were dead, murdered in their beds and buried somewhere within the dark forbidding walls of the Thomas. Thomas hadn't asked on which authority she had found out this information. He rather suspected that if he enquired further then he might not like the answer, and worried that it might end at his own door.

Thomas had come out in support of Richard during Buckingham's rebellion, a rebellion that his wife fully supported and helped finance. She managed to escape with her life after Thomas had intervened. It had actually worked out well for him as Margret was placed under house arrest and her wealth and lands were transferred to his name.

But in recent months, Thomas had begun to have doubts about his king. It could not be contested that Richard had usurped the throne from his nephew, despite the web of lies that had been constructed to suggest the children were illegitimate. Margret kept up a constant stream of promises: yes, he held wealth and a certain degree of power, but what he had now was nothing compared to what he would be awarded if he were step-father to the king.

All he had to do to was help put Margret Beaufort's son on the throne.

It was a tantalising prospect.

Until three hours ago Stanley had never met his step-son. It had been impossible of course, as Henry Tudor had spent the vast majority of life in exile overseas.

But here within the thick walls of the Abbey they had met. It was a place to discuss secrets. Dark secrets. Treason perhaps.

Stanley was impressed with Henry Tudor. He was tall man with an intensity in his eyes. It struck him that he looked more like a king than Richard. As they talked, Tudor appeared thoughtful and intelligent. Never once did he seem arrogant or conceited.

At the end of the meeting he found himself promising his and his brother's forces to Henry's cause.

But, of course, there were the usual Stanley caveats.

The Stanley's would not be publicly declaring their allegiance and they certainly wouldn't be lining up behind Tudor's Welsh Dragon banner. Thomas Stanley liked to play both sides until he was sure how the dice would land. If he had learnt anything it was the importance of backing the winning side.

Stanley's position was also hampered by the fact that Richard held his son and heir, Lord Strange, as a hostage. Richard's letters had become increasingly more threatening in recent days as he demanded that Stanley bring his forces to Leicester to join the rest of the royal army. Stanley's first gambit had been to say that he was stuck in Nottingham with the sweat. Once that had been cured, then his argument was that he couldn't join with Richard's forces because he was holding Whatling Street for the king, thus preventing Henry Tudor from marching from Lichfield down the roman road to London.

Stanley knew that Tudor wasn't easily fooled. Tudor knew that Stanley had promised himself to both men.

But Stanley believed he had given his step-son hope. And if he helped him to victory then the rewards would be immense.

6:57 AM 21st August 1485
Latham House
26 hours and 18 minutes until the death of Richard III

Margret Beaufort was at prayer.

She scratched her shoulder subconsciously. Her coarse hair shirt worn underneath her garments had caused her all manner of personal discomfort over the recent weeks, yet now more than ever was a good time to be close to Christ.

She knew that it couldn't be long until the battle was fought. Any moment now she might receive news.

She had arranged for a string of young messengers from here to wherever her son's army was that day. She sent him letters each day, completely disregarding the terms of her detainment. Her husband wasn't there to prevent her from doing so, not that he would have tried, thought Margret. Her son wasn't as diligent with his replies, but between his and Jasper's communications she had a fair idea of what was occurring. The support of Rhys Ap Thomas was critical to her son's cause and she had given particular thanks when news of this reached her.

Her husband's communications were few and far between. There was little to read in the short messages he sent her. There was nothing in writing that would incriminate him of treason.

Which way would her husband go?

She prayed harder that he would have the wisdom to make the right choice.

OUT NOW!

Printed in Poland
by Amazon Fulfillment
Poland Sp. z o.o., Wrocław